Royalist Political Thought During the French Revolution

Recent Titles in
Contributions to the Study of World History

Medieval Games: Sports and Recreations in Feudal Society
John Marshall Carter

Families in Context: A World History of Population
G. Robina Quale

Waiting for Jerusalem: Surviving the Holocaust in Romania
I. C. Butnaru

Israel's Leadership: From Utopia to Crisis
Jacob Abadi

Christopher Columbus and the Portuguese, 1476–1498
Rebecca Catz

Clinging to Grandeur: British Attitudes and Foreign Policy in the Aftermath of the Second World War
Michael Blackwell

The Legend of the Mutilated Victory: Italy, the Great War, and the Paris Peace Conference, 1915–1919
H. James Burgwyn

Spain in the Nineteenth-Century World: Essays on Spanish Diplomacy, 1789–1898
James W. Cortada, editor

The Entangling Alliance: The United States and European Security, 1950–1993
Ronald E. Powaski

Kings of Celtic Scotland
Benjamin T. Hudson

America's Feeble Weapon: Funding the Marshall Plan in France and Italy, 1948–1950
Chiarella Esposito

The Jews of Medieval France: The Community of Champagne
Emily Taitz

Royalist Political Thought During the French Revolution

JAMES L. OSEN

Contributions to the Study of World History, *Number 47*

GREENWOOD PRESS
Westport, Connecticut • London

Library of Congress Cataloging-in-Publication Data

Osen, James L.
Royalist political thought during the French revolution / James L. Osen.
p. cm.—(Contributions to the study of world history, ISSN 0885–9159 ; no. 47)
Includes bibliographical references and index.
ISBN 0–313–29441–0 (alk. paper)
1. Political science—France—History—18th century. 2. France—History—Revolution, 1789–1799. 3. Monarchy. I. Title. II. Series.
JA84.F8084 1995
320.5—dc20 94–25056

British Library Cataloguing in Publication Data is available.

Library of Congress Catalog Card Number: 94–25056
ISBN: 0–313–29441–0
ISSN: 0885–9159

First published in 1995

Greenwood Press, 88 Post Road West, Westport, CT 06881
An imprint of Greenwood Publishing Group, Inc.

Printed in the United States of America

The paper used in this book complies with the Permanent Paper Standard issued by the National Information Standards Organization (Z39.48–1984).

10 9 8 7 6 5 4 3 2 1

To Professor Robert H. Irrmann,
Mentor and Friend

Contents

Acknowledgments

I have worked on this study of royalist political thought over a long period of time and in the process have accumulated debts to persons and to institutions. The biggest debt is to Robert Irrmann, my department chairman for many years at Beloit College, who helped me obtain an appointment to the Newberry Library, which was key to the development of this project. I found my way through some of that library's 33,000 French Revolution pamphlets thanks to the generous assistance of Bernard E. Wilson of Technical Services. Because the collection was uncatalogued at that time, I knew that if anything happened to Bernie my research would be over. During that year Lawrence W. Towner, the Librarian, Rita T. Fitzgerald, Jane E. Smith, Donald W. Krummel, Paul F. Gehl, and John Aubrey were also very helpful. The Newberry Library is a community of scholars. Other scholars who have been helpful professionally and personally are Jeremy Popkin (who has been particularly generous in sharing his knowledge on this subject), Clarke Garrett, and Oscar Arnal.

I would also like to thank the staff at the British Library, the Bibliothèque nationale, the Bibliothèque de la Ville de Paris, the Memorial Library at the University of Wisconsin-Madison, the Beloit College Library (with special thanks to Chris Nelson), and the Ontonagon (Michigan) Township Library. I also acknowledge ongoing support from the Faculty Development Fund at Beloit College. However, none of these persons nor places is responsible for the results of my research.

At Greenwood Press, I want to thank my copy editor, Leslie C. Treff, who did an especially thorough and efficient job, and the production managers, Melissa Freeman and Lori Blackwell, who kept me on task and made many helpful suggestions. David Heesen and Joan Salzberg in Secretarial Services at Beloit College rendered innumerable services—cheerfully and expertly. And my wife, Meta, did editing and proofreading, and sustained me at every stage during the years of research and writing.

Introduction

This book concentrates on French revolutionary royalist thought. It makes no attempt to trace royalist conspiracies in France, nor does it include those of émigrés abroad, both of which have been treated elsewhere. Royalists were divided between constitutional and absolutist monarchists. This book attempts to provide as complete a study of the absolutists as possible, though it makes some mention of the constitutionalists too. It builds on Paul H. Beik's seminal analysis, *The French Revolution Seen from the Right: Social Theories in Motion, 1789–1799*, which provided a general survey of right-wing opinion. Beik, however, did not include a study of the press, as does this work. I believe, therefore, my study provides the first systematic treatment of the absolutist position.

Chapters are arranged pretty much in a chronological fashion, beginning with early royalist explanations of the causes of the Revolution and continuing through the period of the Directory. The material divides itself naturally between explanations of the causes of the Revolution and defenses of monarchism. At first royalists concentrated on causation. They wanted to find out how and why the government of the Old Regime, which they had thought a viable operation, had been overturned. And their first reaction was that it resulted from some evil outside force. On more sober reflection other royalist commentators came to find fault with the Old Regime and to come up with much more complex schemes of causation. So this book in part is about the creation of an increasingly sophisticated royalist historiography of the causes of the Revolution, which in turn fed into a general understanding of the history of this period.

But more and more royalists concentrated on the faults of the unfolding Revolution and explained how a reformed monarchy would be vastly superior. In the process they not only made a contribution to political thought, they were also preparing arguments for their eventual return to power. Basic political issues were now being discussed, and royalists, along with radicals, moderate republics, liberals, and socialists, were helping set the political agenda for the nineteenth century.

The sources on this subject are rich. I have largely drawn from the extensive collection at the Newberry Library, which has many pamphlets and newspapers, plus secondary materials on the subject. Unfortunately, however, only the anonymous pamphlets are catalogued. For other primary sources one must work indirectly through Martin and Walter, and make some stabs in the dark. Other materials came from the excellent collections at the Bibliothèque nationale and the British Library.

The main problem I encountered studying this subject was the suppression of royalist publications whenever the Revolution entered a particularly radical phase. And it must be said that royalists often were not innocent victims. They frequently called for counter-revolution and retribution, even when France was in the midst of war. Hence on the period of the Terror, 1793–1794, I have had to rely on accounts published by royalists who were abroad. Similarly there are gaps during periods of the Directory. Royalist journalists were ingenious in their attempts to escape government prohibitions: they changed the name of their paper, somtimes frequently, and they changed staffs. But in the end they did not enjoy freedom of publication, and much was lost.

CHAPTER I

Early Royalist Explanations of the Causes of the French Revolution

French monarchists, whose world had been turned upside down, were preoccupied with the causes of the French Revolution. In explaining what had gone wrong, they began by saying that there was nothing wrong with the government of the Old Regime. The French Revolution, they thought, came about simply because outside forces had engaged in a conspiracy, resulting in the overthrow of the old order and the substitution of a reign of terror and chaos. But, in time, some became increasingly sophisticated in their analysis, admitted that there were some flaws in the monarchy, identified problems to rectify before a restoration of the monarchy and in the process made a contribution to historiography and to the explanation of historical causation.

One of the first accounts came from the abbé Jean Baptiste Du Voisin (1744–1813), canon of Laon, in *La France chrétienne, juste et vraiment libre* of 1789.[1] Du Voisin began with the divine right of kings, thought the clergy should support the King, and believed that any rapid changes in the constitution would be full of peril:

> Political governments are good, they are necessary only for the maintenance of peace; and peace can be affirmed only by the stability of governments. A constitution that could be freely changed every day is no better than the condition of the savages and the denial of government. It is worth less because this perpetual mutuality would multiply the subjects of discord, it would add a teeming and inexhaustible cause to the divisions always springing up again, to the miseries and the disorders that afflict scattered families, who do not live in society. If one could pass as one wished from one form of government to another, it would be to unite to divide, to torment oneself, to become mutually impoverished and destroy each other.[2]

So any change that took place had to be done very gradually.

The only indication Du Voisin gave that there was something wrong with the Old Regime was his advocacy of regular meetings of the Estates-General.[3]

Furthermore he proposed a national council, drawn from representatives of the three orders, which would meet in permanent session and daily "receive the complaints and requests of the cities, the communities, the corps and the individuals of the entire kingdom . . . to communicate these complaints and requests to the throne, to enlighten the decision of authority, and provide accurately a justified response to the interested parties. . . ."[4] Otherwise things should be left as they were.

The most famous early French royalist account of the causes of the French Revolution came from the abbé Augustin de Barruel (1741–1820), who began his explanation in 1789 with *La patriote véridique, ou discours sur les vraies causes de la révolution actuelle*, continued it in 1791 in *Question nationale sur l'autorité*, took up the subject again in *Histoire du clergé pendant la Révolution françoise* of 1793, and expanded on it in his most famous work, *Mémoires pour servir à l'histoire du jacobinisme,* 1797–1798.

Barruel, editor of the *Journal ecclésiastique ou Bibliothèque raisonnée des sciences ecclésiastiques* from 1788 to 1792 and a representative of the clergy at the Estates-General,[5] took little time to make up his mind about the causes of the French Revolution. In *La patriote véridique*, which appeared first in the *Journal ecclésiastique* beginning in January of 1789 and which Paul Beik thought was completed before June or July of that year,[6] he sought to demonstrate that the causes of the French Revolution were the depravity of public morality and the progress of the ideas of the philosophes, which had come about, above all, because of the abuses of the clergy.[7]

First of all, Barruel argued that a people without religion and morality would always face ruin. Dogma always had to support the throne, tie the subjects to the sovereign, and give sanction to the laws. Without these principles, "the state has no base, the wicked no restraint, and the law no force."[8]

As far as the deficit was concerned, it was not the fault of Louis XVI, who loved his people too much to be a friend of luxury. The evil was in the court, but it originated in the villages, the provinces, in all the vice that reigned in the state. People were astonished at the deficit, but they should have realized that at the capital almost everyone looked to the public treasury to provide for his passions.[9]

The only fundamental remedy for the state of affairs was a return to religion, which would, "prescribe just sacrifices to the rich, respect to the people, justice to the princes, obedience to the subjects, integrity to the magistrates, faithfulness to ministers and administrators, and charity, love, peace, and concord to all. Religion, by retaining each in his duties, would make order reign everywhere and make the state happy by the virtue of all."[10]

The basic problem was the weakness of the clergy, who had allowed religion and morality to decline and the ideas of the philosophes to spread. Their lives had discredited their doctrines. They had a holy calling, but their morality was profane. Hence their teachings did not inspire the respect that virtue would have produced. They had reasoned and written in favor of their dogmas, which was necessary, but it was not enough. What they had to do was set a good example of Christian humility, poverty, kindness, virtue, and sincere piety. These, he said, were their true arms. So the difficulty stemmed ultimately, not from the philosophes, but from the clergy.[11]

By 1791, in his *Question nationale sur l'autorité et sur les droits du peuple dans le gouvernement*, Barruel had dug in his heels in defense of absolute monarchy and denied that there was any right of revolution. No changes could be made in the old monarchy without the "*unanimous* consent of the sovereign and all the individuals in the nation."[12] And, as far as the causes of the Revolution were concerned, there was no longer any criticism of the Old Regime or of the Church. By this time he was well on his way to formulating a conspiracy theory, and the philosophes were the centerpiece of it. "These days of tempest were produced by the so-called philosophers, who only knew how to assemble clouds and prepare storms, and who produced confusion and disorder in the state, after having confused, mixed up, and turned upside down all notions of true philosophy."[13]

After his departure from France in September of 1792, Barruel wrote *Histoire du clergé pendant la Révolution française*. Here he continued his indictment of the philosophes and broadened his attack to include the Physiocrats. He thought that they had long conspired to overthrow the throne and the altar. Those who aimed primarily at replacing the monarchy were not totally opposed to all religion, which they thought was good for the people, though they did not want to follow it themselves. But they wanted to eliminate Catholicism because it would be incompatible with the type of government they wanted to establish. The leader of these political philosophes, he said, was Mirabeau the elder. Others concentrated their fire on the Church. According to Barruel, the result was the attack on the State and the Church that took place during the French Revolution.[14]

But by far the most famous formulation of the conspiracy theory of the causes of the French Revolution came in his *Mémoires pour servir à l'histoire du jacobinisme* (4 vols., 1797–98), which caused a sensation.[15] "The result of our research, corroborated by proofs drawn from the records of the Jacobins, and of their first masters, has been, that this sect with its conspiracies is in itself no other than the coalition of a triple sect, of a triple conspiracy, in which, long before the revolution, the overthrow of the altar, the ruin of the throne, and the dissolution of all civil society had been debated and resolved on."[16]

The first conspiracy, he said, consisted of the philosophes, who attacked Christianity. Shortly thereafter they formed a rebellion against kings and were joined in their attack by the Freemasons, who were opposed to both Christianity and monarchy. The Spiritualists, who were against every religion and every government, formed the third branch. These three then joined to make up the Jacobins, who proceeded to launch their assault against God, the King, and society itself during the French Revolution.[17]

This conspiracy theory had a powerful impact and a long currency because it provided a simple, clear, and neat explanation of what had gone wrong in a period of great upheaval. Reduced to its barest minimum—the French Revolution was the fault of Rousseau—it was one that all could understand. It was especially attractive to royalists because it whitewashed the Old Regime—there was nothing wrong with the government or the society—who were undermined by an outside conspiracy. And it was attractive to the Church. According to Barruel, both church and state had been attacked by the same forces; now they must stand together.

Other accounts written by absolutists between 1789 and 1791 included one by Antoine Rivarol (1753–1801) that appeared in the royalist newspaper *Journal Politique National*, edited by the abbé Sabatier de Castres. While denying that the philosophes themselves were a direct cause of the Revolution, Rivarol argued that popularizations of their writings did play an important part:

> It is indisputable that the Books of the Philosophes did not do anything by themselves since the People did not read them and did not know them. But it is no less true that they were very harmful by all the Books that they inspired and that the People very well understood. A brochure such as the *Orateur aux États Généraux*, which is only a disgusting paraphrase of several lines of the *Social Contract*, was spread incredibly among the lower class who had never read the *Social Contract*. In other times a book which did not pass through the antechamber was not dangerous; today in effect there are only those who do not leave the antechambers that are truly to be feared. In this one must admire the philosophes who write with elevation to correct Governments and not to overthrow them, to help the people and not to raise them up. But the Governments scorned the voice of the great Writers and gave time to little spirits to begin works of Genius and to put them at the disposal of the Populace.[18]

This theory, considerably more sophisticated than Barruel's, foreshadows Sénac de Meilhan's charge that the government was too passive and R. R. Palmer's remark that the failure of the Old Regime was in part a failure of public relations.[19]

Another account appeared in an anonymous pamphlet of 1790, *Nécessité d'une contre-révolution*, which argued that modern philosophy was one of the causes of the Revolution. According to the pamphleteer, it had introduced the principle of revolt and raised against the King a people who before had respected him and regarded him as sacrosanct.[20]

This explanation went on to assert that many of the problems had developed during the reign of Louis XV; "the vessel of the state was beaten by the most horrible storms when he [Louis XVI] took the helm. And, instead of breaking it against the rocks, he sustained it against the furor of the waves and employed all his prudence to prevent it from being shipwrecked." But it suggested that one of the problems was the weakness of Louis XVI; "he would have always been master if he had been a tyrant, and he is today a slave for having been too good."[21]

Finally the pamphlet reserved special criticism for Maurepas, whom it described as an "eighty-year-old skeleton," who had been "pulled from the bottom of his tomb" and who presented France with "the spectacle of an old child." This "old imbecile" was the one responsible for restoring "the companies of brigands" (the parlements), who so justly had been chased from power by Louis XV.[22]

The last of these works is Chaillon de Jonville's *La Révolution de France prophétisée*, published in 1791. While not nearly as sophisticated as Sénac de Meilhan's version, it was more complex than any other accounts considered during this period. Augustin Jean François Chaillon de Jonville (1733–1807) became a counselor to the parlement of Paris at the age of 19, then was made master of requests, and in 1765 was one of the commissioners named to judge Louis de La Chalotais, the procurer general of the parlement of Brittany. At the approach of the Revolution he published apologies for absolute monarchy[23] and emigrated in 1789.[24]

Chaillon de Jonville began his explanation of the Revolution with the first ministry of Necker. Necker was the villain; he was the one who borrowed millions so that the American insurgents could rebel against their lawful king. This policy dishonored and eventually ruined France, and was the cause of the deficit and all the evils that flowed from it.[25]

Then Chaillon de Jonville singled out Lamoignon, named guardian of the seals in 1787. Lamoignon was described as being two-faced, inconsistent, a slave to ambition, and unworthy of the name he bore. In a political move this old parlementary opponent of the kings was selected only because the ministers believed that they needed the support of the parlements. According to Chaillon, it was like letting the Trojan horse into the gate. Chaillon's argument demonstrated how absolutists saw parlementary opposition leading to the Revolution. Chaillon de Jonville also had poisonous things to say about Loménie de Brienne. So the gist of the first section of his work is that Louis XVI was fine, but he was betrayed by bad ministers.[26]

The second point, in a sulphurous work, is that the Revolution stemmed from the ideas of the philosophes, ". . . and the philosophes printed all their systematic and disturbing follies, and they were wrong; they were read, and that was wrong; and Mr. Necker, far from stopping them in their mistaken course, invited them in the name of the King to instruct the throne with their wisdom, and he was very wrong."[27]

But Chaillon de Jonville protested that Rousseau, whose ideas served as a pretext for the Revolution, actually had been falsely interpreted and that his principles were opposed to all the decrees of the Assembly.[28]

True philosophy, Chaillon de Jonville argued, was based on the principles of religion, hierarchy, and humanity, which assured the true happiness of the state. "True philosophy exhorts . . . all the French to maintain their loyalty, their sincerity, their principle of honor . . . and above all that love for their Kings, which in all times is confounded in their hearts with love of their country. . . ."[29] True philosophy, he went on, loves liberty, but hates license, especially that of the press. In fact, license in the press, he thought, had produced all the recent troubles. True philosophy called for the sanction of the law against all uprisings and heavy punishments against all offenders.[30]

Having dealt with the two sides of philosophy, Jonville turned his attention to the role of Necker on his return to power in 1788–1789. Besides inviting the philosophes to instruct the government, as previously noted, against the advice of the parlements, the Assembly of the Notables, the council of the King and the King himself, he then organized the Estates-General in a fashion directly opposite to the system of 1614. That was the second cause of the troubles. The third cause was Necker's doubling of the Third Estate.[31]

Next, when Louis XVI tried to make a last stand at the Royal Session on June 23, 1789, Necker let his opposition be known and even had the temerity to refuse to attend the session.[32] Finally, after his dismissal on July 7, 1789, he and his followers unleashed civil war in France.[33]

As the Revolution reached the boiling point, Chaillon de Jonville also faulted Louis XVI and his ministers, who failed to act decisively at the right moment. All they had to do, he thought, was to announce on the morning of July 12, 1789, that they only wanted to "lay hands on the rebels, disperse the brigands, reassure the credulous inhabitants, and above all protect the artisans." Somehow this would have stopped the disorder. But, unfortunately, they did not, so once again the weakness and the indecisiveness of Louis XVI were important factors. In the meantime their foes, led by the duc d'Orléans, organized insurrections in Paris and the provinces and succeeded in overthrowing the regime.[34]

But even this was not enough to account for what had occurred, so Chaillon de Jonville, in the final analysis, fell back on a providential explanation. "And all these things took place with the permission of God, perhaps even through his vengeance because the human spirit, no matter how villainous the conspirators were, is too weak, too limited, to have predicted, calculated, even wished from the beginning all that happened. The activity of the conspirators, the inertia of honest men, the slumber of the military, the lethargy of the King and his good council, nothing of any of that was natural."[35]

The royalist press picked up the same theme. *L'Ami du Roi* of the abbé Royou argued that "Voltaire and Rousseau were for France devastating scourges sent by divine anger." And about the same time the *Journal de la Cour et de la Ville* said that God allowed the Revolution to take place to teach the people that the so-called wisdom of the philosophes was nothing more than "madness and thick darkness."[36]

Other accounts in the right-wing press between 1789 and 1792 reflected, amplified, and embellished the views contained in royalist pamphlets and books. Most subscribed to the conspiracy theory of history: hostile outside forces had undermined a regime that basically was good and just. Much of this press pointed the finger of blame at the philosophes, who had undermined public morality by their attacks on religion. And the journalists emphasized that this had been going on for a long time. The plot had included Rousseau, d'Alembert, Diderot, Turgot, and others, who were allowed to spread their propaganda in spite of warnings of the consequences.[37]

Other journals, including the *Gazette de Paris*, the *Annales monarchiques*, the *Journal Général de France*, and the *Journal du peuple*, while upholding the theory of a plot, emphasized the subversive role played by French Protestants. While both philosophes and Protestants placed conscience before authority, Protestants were republicans, who planned the overthrow of the King and of Catholicism in their secret consistories.[38]

Since this was the case, the abbé Royou argued strongly against a policy of religious tolerance. "The Catholic religion is and must be intolerant by its very essence; one of its principle dogmas is that every other cult is reproved by the Supreme Being. Now, how can it be supposed that religious men can live in peace with those whom they regard as the enemies of their God?" Religious diversity, he thought, would lead either to civil war or to religious apathy, each of which would be destructive of the country and its people.[39]

And, springing from the same soil as Protestantism, the right-wingers pointed the finger of blame at the Masonic movement. One of the first to identify them was Du Rozoi in *La Gazette de Paris* of October 31, 1790:

> Equality between brothers, abolition of ranks, signs of recognition, passwords in the Assemblies and for admittance into the mysteries, unity from one end to the other, a *federative Republic*; there is the system, the base, the spirit, and the harmonious constitution of *Masonry*. This observation, more important perhaps than one realizes, is so true, that in these days of crime, of delirium, and of insurrection when blood was flowing, when heads marched on the Place de Grève at the end of pikes, one could force one's way through the crowds of People drunk with fury and one could enter the Hotel de Ville by means of masonic signs. All those who appeared first in the Theater of the Revolution were the Chiefs of Lodges.[40]

Other conservative journalists took up the same theme in their favorable reviews of abbé Lefranc's *Le Voile levé pour les curieux* of 1789 and later of his *Conjuration contre la religion catholique et les souverains* of 1792, which identified Masonry as the problem. Montjoie in his *Ami du Roi* reviewed these books at length, equated the rites of the National Assembly with those of the Freemasons, and argued that the Masonic principles of liberty and equality had permeated the Revolution.[41]

The *Journal à deux liards* not only showed the similarity between Masonic and revolutionary forms and argued that Masonry was the cause of all the troubles in Europe, but pointed out that the duc d'Orléans, the Masonic Grand

Master, was "the very man suspected of being the Chief of the faction which has plunged us into our present troubles."[42]

Others, however, named Necker as the problem. Necker was a likely target because he had advised the King during the crisis of 1788–1789, because he was a Protestant, and because he was a foreigner. The Right then thought of itself as the truly patriotic party and identified the Left with foreign subversives. Indeed, the Right considered the ideas of all of its enemies, including the Protestants, the Freemasons, and even the philosophes as essentially foreign in origin, alien to French traditions, and destructive of French institutions.[43]

Rivarol in the *Journal Politique National* again probed deeper. He saw Necker only as the champion of the financiers, who were the ones responsible for the collapse of the monarchy. The "King's creditors" had destroyed him. The stock exchange ruled Paris, Paris ruled France, and Necker did everything he could to help his financial cronies. France on the eve of the Revolution had only two choices: either to compete with Britain in commerce, which it could not do, or to declare bankruptcy, which would have hurt Parisian financial interests, but would have saved the rest of the country. France owed speculators nothing.

Rivarol's attitude indicated a general prejudice of the Right in favor of landed interests against the so-called corruption of the cities. The Right tended to prefer birth and inheritance to individual achievement and upward mobility. Businessmen, the vile bourgeoisie, took their economics from the physiocrats and their morality from the philosophes and were detestable.[44]

Finally, once the Revolution began, the extreme right-wing press, like the abbé Barruel, argued that all the factors came together in the Jacobin Clubs. For example the abbé Royou reported in the *Ami du Roi* that in the anti-monarchical demonstration of July 17, 1791, the participants were simply the blind instruments of the Jacobins. The people, according to Royou, usually were quiescent and very indifferent to political questions. They only budged when they had been roused and bribed. Investigators, Royou said, found the cause of popular uprisings to be the Jacobin Clubs, and the discourses and the writings of Jacobins, who incited the populace to destroy the kingdom.[45]

It was Gabriel Sénac de Meilhan (1736–1803) who early in the Revolution came up with the most sophisticated explanation of its causes. Sénac de Meilhan had served as an intendant since 1766. A correspondent of Voltaire and an ally of Turgot and the physiocrats, he opposed Necker's candidacy for the finance ministry in 1776, and in 1787 he answered Necker's *Compte rendu* with his own *Considérations sur les richesses et le luxe*, which followed physiocratic principles. Thereafter he was an unsuccessful candidate to become Controller General of Finance. Sénac de Meilhan favored the calling of the Estates-General because he thought it would help restore the French monarchy. Though he was opposed to the doubling of the Third Estate, he hoped for a new constitution in which royal power would be balanced by that of representatives in the style of Montesquieu and the English constitution. But the course of the Revolution soon disappointed him and made him uneasy. In 1790 he resigned his intendancy and went into exile.[46]

At Aix-la-Chapelle that summer and fall he wrote his first explanation of what had gone wrong, *Des Principes et des causes de la Révolution en France*. He began with abuses of the government under the reign of Louis XV, and he did not whitewash the Old Regime. His first point was that Louis XV had been much too inaccessible. Hence he was unable to become acquainted with public servants, judge their abilities, and win their esteem. In fact, he was as cut off as if he were a despot, and Sénac de Meilhan pointed out that it was in despotic countries that revolutions occurred most frequently. And, while Louis XV devoted himself to his pleasures, respect for the monarch diminished and opposition to his authority increased. The King lacked a will, and his ministers had no plans nor principles.[47]

Moreover, Sénac argued that the religious quarrels during the reign of Louis XV were handled badly.[48] The parlements, eager to restore the Jansenists, turned against the Jesuits. They were aided by men of letters, who succeeded in stirring public opinion up against the Jesuit order. As a result the King was powerless to help them. Sénac considered their expulsion a blow to royal authority. It was, he said, a victory for the parlements against the government, which encouraged the courts to resist in other areas.[49]

By the end of the reign of Louis XV things had become very bad indeed. "The morals of the court were irregular. . . . The ministers, devoted to the mistress, were absolute, corrupt and uninformed. The people were charged with taxes, and the inequality of the distribution of the charges was more oppressive than their excess."[50]

After further travels in Italy, Russia, and Austria, Sénac de Meilhan settled down for a while in 1794 and 1795, first at Brandenburg and then at Brunswick. There he composed his second major work on the coming of the French Revolution, *Du gouvernement, des moeurs, et des conditions en France, avant la révolution* in 1795.[51]

In this work, as far as the abuses under the Old Regime were concerned, he made the following judgment: "I am far from thinking that the Government was without abuses, but they were not as numerous and were not strong enough to destroy or paralyze the inalterable principles of prosperity that comprised this powerful Empire."[52]

But he did underline the fact that there were weaknesses in the ministry during the latter years of the reign of Louis XV. Whereas Louis XIV had limited power to lesser nobles who did not have a powerful entourage behind them, now, after the disgrace of the marquis d'Argenson and Jean Baptiste Machault,[53] more military officers and more men of the court were elevated to the ministry. And, once there, they began to make all kinds of changes, which created confusion and had the effect of lessening military discipline. What we have here is a hint of the notion of the aristocratic resurgence of the eighteenth century, but Sénac made it clear that this institutional weakness was not enough by itself to account for the French Revolution.[54]

When Sénac de Meilhan contemplated the causes of the French Revolution, unlike the abbé Barruel, he denied that the writings of the philosophes were a basic factor. Though he admitted that they might have had some influence, as early as 1795 he argued that it had been grossly exaggerated. Sénac, who had known the philosophes and the physiocrats and was sympathetic to their work, said that although Voltaire certainly did stand in the way of religion, he did not have anything to do with the business of the government and, in any case, was more favorable than unfavorable to the monarchy. Sénac described the works of Montesquieu as "apologies for the monarchy, the nobility, and the Parlements." Though the *Social Contract* of Rousseau did advocate unlimited liberty, which was later adopted, this work was so heavy and abstract that few people read and understood it. The same could be said for the writings of Mably. What actually happened, according to Sénac, was that after the Revolution had taken place people looked back in the writings of Mably, Rousseau, and others to find support for the new system which had been arrived at independently.[55]

As Sénac de Meilhan assessed the causes of the French Revolution, not only did he hint at the aristocratic resurgence, but he also gave some suggestion that behind it lay the threat to the aristocrats posed by the growing importance of wealth: "The domination of wealth, and the effects that result from it, when nothing serves as a counterweight to it, are among the causes of the alteration of the government."[56] Socially he took a very conservative tack: it was essential that each of the orders that made up the government conserve its place. But the growth of wealth upset the old order and undermined the government that was based on it. Equality began to replace aristocracy, and the rich looked forward to a republican regime that would favor them.[57]

Another cause contributing to the French Revolution, Sénac thought, was the unstable character of the French people. Looking back from 1795, he said that, whereas in another place the same factors might have had no effect, in France they led to a general conflagration. "Seduced, five years ago, by the ideas of liberty, this People . . . *passed beyond the bounds of liberty*. Julius Caesar knew the character of the inhabitants of Gaul well, when he said . . . it is a Nation too ferocious to be free."[58] So Sénac emphasized that the government was far from being oppressive. There was no excess of abuses, but rather a genetic defect in French character which made the French prone to Revolution.[59]

He next examined the causes during the reign of Louis XVI. The chief thing he emphasized here, mainly in *Des principes et des causes de la Révolution en France* of 1790, was the instability and general inability of the ministers. "They contented themselves with providing for the moment; they had no plans, no views, and they lacked the sense of government."[60] The ministry of finance, he said, was the worst of all. Controllers General came and went, and most concerned themselves only with the measures necessary to get by during their short tenure.[61]

One of the worst ministers, he believed, was Maurepas, who thought only of his own reputation and of his hatred of Louis XV, who had dismissed him. He restored the parlements to win public favor and to satisfy his resentment against the former king. A statesman would have behaved differently: he would have profited from the judicial revolution that had been accomplished. He would have seen that the old magistrates were well treated, consolidated the position of the new courts, and thereby assured peace in France for the next fifty years. And he would have been able to achieve important reforms, without being checked by "the pretensions, the prejudices, and the routine" of the old judges. But "the desire for a passing success carried him away; the Parlements were re-established and believed themselves forever immovable."[62]

One of the important causes of the Revolution, according to Sénac de Meilhan, was the fall of Turgot, who was Sénac's sole hero among the ministers of Louis XVI. Although Sénac, who had associated with Turgot, looked on his reform efforts from a very favorable point of view, he did not overlook his flaws. Sénac found Turgot too zealous and too prone to stir people up. By explaining his edicts, he provoked others to state their opinions on the question at hand.[63] But Sénac admired Turgot's principles.[64] As it was, Turgot was checked by all his enemies, who blocked his reforms because of their own vested interests.[65]

As Sénac assessed the ministers of Louis XVI, he found that Necker was the very worst and also one of the most important causes of the French Revolution. Sénac's evaluation of Necker, the successor of the noble Turgot, was harsh:

> More fatal to France than Cromwell was to England, he did not have an ambition that subdued by its audacity, which dazzled by its vast undertakings. He overthrew the state, without having a fixed plan, by following from day to day the outbursts of his vanity. Administrator of finance without ability and without doctrine, man of state without views, supporter of despotism in his writings, timid republican in his conduct, more in love of applause than with true glory, vacillating in his opinions, uncertain in his course, he finished by discontenting all the parties, which he had caressed in turn.[66]

As Minister of Finance from 1776 to 1781 he seemed to be a miracle worker: by his wizardry he was able to wage war without levying taxes! While actually preparing France for inevitable bankruptcy, he prided himself on having achieved a state of momentary prosperity.[67]

Out of office he became an even greater menace because a party formed around him determined to criticize all the operations of the government. A direct line connected this opposition, according to Sénac, with the coming of the French Revolution. Factions arose against the government, public opinion was stirred up, the regime was discredited, the Estates-General called, and the monarchy subverted.[68]

Sénac de Meilhan next considered the effects of the French intervention in the American War for Independence. The French in America, he said, became imbued with republican principles and with popularity. As a result, the submission of the army to the King was weakened. France came out of the war with huge debts, an immense loss of life, and absolutely no advantages for France. "The war in America thus subverted at the same time, in France, men's minds and the public fortune."[69]

After referring to the diamond necklace affair, which he said prejudiced minds against the regime,[70] Sénac said that in the last years of the Old Regime the government foolishly permitted political clubs to exist. They discussed all the political questions of the day, circulated opinions and news rapidly, and inflamed public opinion. Several years later, when they wanted to suppress the clubs, the ministers no longer had enough authority to do so.[71]

After the government failed to raise taxes during the American Revolution, it found that it could not do so in peacetime because the necessity was unclear. So it continued Necker's mistaken policy of borrowing until it could borrow no more. Then it called the Assembly of Notables in 1787 and presented new programs to it. But Calonne's reform program was undermined by the partisans of Necker, who blocked any action.[72]

By 1788 the parlement of Paris had become so concerned about the state of affairs and so carried away by the current of opinion that it asserted only the representatives of the nation, meeting in the Estates-General, had the right to consent to taxes.

At this point Loménie de Brienne had the very poor judgment to agree, although he tried to temporize by putting off the meeting until some time in the future. He thus invited people to write about the form and the nature of the Estates-General and to raise questions about the rights of the monarch and those of the people. The discussion, as it unfolded, was not just concerned with reforming old abuses, but with changing the very form of the government itself. Loménie de Brienne, however, remained blind to the dangers. He did not realize that none of the interested parties would help him re-establish the government's financial position because the disarray made a meeting of the Assembly necessary.[73]

Behind the parlement, of course, stood the aristocrats, who were delighted at the establishment of provincial estates, which flattered their self-esteem by giving them an opportunity to participate in administrative affairs. They wanted to increase their influence in the provinces by drawing on their connection with the court and win a greater role at the court by drawing on their influence in the provinces. All the while they would undercut the power of the ministers. "These aristocrats were the true authors of the revolution. They inflamed tempers in the

Capital and the Provinces by their example and their discourse and then could not stop or slow down the movement that they had excited."[74]

Sénac further observed that members of the Third Estate also wanted an Estates-General so they could take part and make a name for themselves, especially since they had a limited role and therefore had everything to gain and nothing to lose. The idea in essence is that of a middle-class revolution. And, he said, some members of the nobility and the Third Estate hoped to establish a hereditary upper house, where they could play an exalted role.[75]

Sénac argued that even at this late date things might have turned out all right if the meeting of the Estates-General had been carefully planned and managed. But nothing was done.[76] Once the meeting assembled, the government should have employed the means at hand to influence the Estates-General. This would not have been difficult because most of the members were only interested in "playing a role, acquiring a reputation, and procuring some personal advantages for themselves."[77]

In these circumstances, the recall of Necker to power in August of 1788 was, according to Sénac, the final cause of the French Revolution. "From this moment he dreamed about becoming a national minister and was more occupied in caressing the multitude than in maintaining the authority of the King."[78]

The final blow, more an effect than a cause, came when the army proved unreliable. There had been too many changes in personnel and in rules—especially the order of 1781 that officers had to have four generations of nobility. These changes alienated the Third Estate from the nobility, undermined the army, and favored the course of the French Revolution.[79]

Sénac de Meilhan's explanation has a lot to recommend it. It is a definite step beyond the theory that the Old Regime was all right and was just overcome by an outside conspiracy. Sénac is careful to point out government mistakes when he discovers them. Moreover he denies that the ideas of the philosophes played a role. He distinguishes between the various philosophes and says that many of their ideas were favorable to the monarchy. And he points out that, after the fact, revolutionaries looked back at the philosophes to try to buttress the positions they had already taken.

Sénac is good at depicting the political naïveté of the Old Regime, which seemed to think that things would go on forever as they had been, without the government bestirring itself to meet crises, make reforms, or challenge opponents. Although he cannot seem to make up his mind about whether the government should have gone public in explaining and defending its policies, and although it is questionable if the state could or should have tried to close political clubs and censor the press, at least he recognizes that a challenge was posed and not met.

Probably Sénac's most important contribution was his assessment of the role played by the nobility in the revolutionary ferment. He provided some indication that wealth was coming to play a more important role than ever before and, though Sénac himself wanted to stick to the old political and social order, that members of the middle class were not willing to keep to their place or let the nobles dominate them.

Another significant explanation is the effect of the French intervention in the American War for Independence. The war certainly affected French finances adversely and contemporary scholarship[80] has brought out the ideological connection between this war and the French Revolution. And Sénac's discussion on the decline of loyalty in the army, though perhaps more of an effect than a cause, is important in explaining how the Revolution could succeed.

On some points, however, Sénac seems to give the wrong emphasis or shoot at the wrong target. Although the calling of the Estates-General certainly did open up the debate and led to the Revolution, it is not clear, after the refusal of the parlements to approve taxes, how it could have been avoided and, once called, it remains a question whether it could have been managed as easily as Sénac assumed. He also appears very harsh on the ministers: except for Turgot, almost all of them were misguided and ineffective, and Necker was nefarious.

On one point he may have missed the mark entirely. It remains doubtful whether the character of the French people as a whole was an essential precondition for Revolution. His remarks about individuals and about groups, such as the nobility and the middle class, appear more salient. Nevertheless, in spite of these flaws, his explanation, first stated a year after the beginning of the Revolution, remains remarkable, especially when compared to those of his contemporaries.

But they too made some contribution. The abbé Barruel began to formulate the idea that the French Revolution was the fault of Rousseau and the philosophes as early as 1791. While this idea is now generally rejected, it eventually did stimulate scholarship on the relationship between ideas and history. And it was denied within the right-wing camp itself at the same time. And while there was a tendency for royalists to absolve the Old Regime of all responsibility, some, as early as 1790, did admit that government was weak and ineffective.

Furthermore, there was a tendency, as seen in Barruel in 1789, for royalists to link religion, morality, and the defense of the political and social order. When the dust began to settle from the French Revolution and Napoleon, these connections began to be emphasized, not only by conservatives, but also by liberals, who were anxious to avoid cataclysmic revolutionary upheavals in the future.

In a related area, French monarchists at this time, like the abbé Du Voisin in 1789, began to stress that any changes that took place should be made gradually. Otherwise the consequence would be chaos, anarchy, civil war, and destruction. The French Revolution taught the wisdom of this observation to many political commentators, both liberal and conservative, and it became a common belief in the first half of the nineteenth century. The organic theory of history is identified with Burke, but it had independent French sources too, forged in the crucible of the Revolution.

Therefore some of these early French conservatives moved beyond the conspiracy theory of history to more complex explanations of the causes of the French Revolution. In the process they helped begin the historiography on this period and made a contribution to explaining historical causation. They also participated in reformulating basic religious, political, and social questions, and came up with ideas that fed into the search for a new principle of political authority.[81]

NOTES

An earlier and shorter version of this chapter appeared as "Early French Conservatives Explain the Causes of the French Revolution," in *Proceedings of the Consortium on Revolutionary Europe*, 15 (1985), 265–80.

1. *Nouvelle Biographie Générale*, 15 (1856), cols. 567–68.

2. [Jean Baptiste Du Voisin] *La France chrétienne, juste et vraiment libre* (n.p., 1789), 158–89.

3. Paul H. Beik, *The French Revolution Seen from the Right: Social Theories in Motion, 1789–1799* (Philadelphia, 1956).

4. Du Voisin, *La France chrétienne*, 151.

5. *Dictionnaire de biographie française*, V (1951), col. 627; Fernand Baldensperger, *Le mouvement des idées dans l'émigration française (1789–1815)* (Paris, 1924), II, 20.

6. Beik, *The French Revolution Seen from the Right*, 20.

7. abbé Augustin de Barruel, *La patriote véridique, ou discours sur les vraies causes de la révolution actuelle* (Paris, 1789), iii.

8. Ibid., 10–11.

9. Ibid., 24.

10. Ibid., 32.

11. Ibid., 57–58.

12. Beik, *The French Revolution Seen from the Right*, 47.

13. *Question nationale sur l'autorité et sur les droits du peuple dans le gouvernement* (Paris, 1791), 44.

14. *Histoire du clergé pendant la révolution françoise*; Ouvrage dedié à la nation angloise (Londres, 1793) 3, 5–7.

15. Baldensperger says that it was so powerful and effective that it overrode all criticism.

> In vain, Joseph de Maistre expressed reservations, knowing that the Masonic liberalism of the century could not be implicated in a common accusation with anarchical theories. In vain, Mallet du Pan exonerated Voltaire from having been part of a "plot." In vain, the readers of Montesquieu protested in the name of the social conservatism evident in that writer. The constitutional monarchists were indignant in vain that one could cover the sans-culottes and the constitutionals with the same reprobation. Vain rectifications? *Paris [pendant l'année 1798]* of [Jean Gabriel] Peltier exhumed, on November 30, 1798, a letter of compliments addressed on his deathbed, May 1, 1797, by Burke to the author, announcing that the work "would be an epoque in the history of men."

Fernand Baldensperger, *Le mouvement des idées dans l'émigration française*, II, 24.

Mounier was among those who attempted to take Barruel on. He argued:

they [modern philosophers] have helped spread in all classes the hatred of arbitrary power. But philosophy has no connection with the circumstances that produced the revolution. The crimes and the miseries were principally the effects of the composition of the Orders, the imprudence of the court, the ignorance of political principles, and the corruption of morals. . . . it is also just to attribute a very large [part] to the errors of those who are not philosophes, to the resistance of those who tried to maintain the old abuses and to revive the prejudices destroyed by the luminaries of the eighteen century.

Jean Joseph Mounier, *De l'influence attribuée aux philosophes, aux francs maçons et aux illuminés, sur la révolution de France* (Paris, 1822), 122. The first edition dated from 1801.

16. *Memoirs, illustrating the History of Jacobinism*, a translation from the French of the abbé Barruel . . . (London, 1797), I, xxi.

17. Ibid., I, xxii–xxiii.

18. *Journal Politique-Nationale*, I (13) (August 9, 1789): 4–5.

19. This reminds one of R. R. Palmer's argument that the failure of the Old Regime was in part a failure of public relations:

The French parlements after the death of Louis XIV, and increasingly as the eighteenth century went on, adopted the practice of publishing their remonstrances, or formal protests, against actions taken by the royal government. These published remonstrances were of great importance in the formation of public opinion. For the first time, the interested person could now obtain some kind of information on matters of current practical politics. . . . The government, however, insisted on the maintenance of administrative privacy, or secrecy, in its affairs. . . . The parlements and their allies always managed to express their views. But no one in authority within the government ever tried to explain their policies to the public. . . .

Since the actual though unknown policies of the French government were often perfectly justifiable, and could have been made to appeal to important segments of the French population, it may be said that the main victim of the withholding of public information was the French monarchy itself, and that its failure was a failure of public relations

R. R. Palmer, *The Age of Democratic Revolution. A Political History of Europe and America, 1760–1800*, Vol. I (Princeton, 1959), 86–87.

20. *Necéssité d'une contre-révolution, prouvée par le décret de l'Assemblée prétendue nationale* . . . (Aux Thuileries, 1790), 2.

21. Ibid., 32–33.

22. Ibid., 65.

23. *Apologie de la constitution françoise; ou États républicains et monarchiques, comparés dans les Histoires de Rome et de France* (n.p., 1789), 2 vols.; *Le Vraie philosophie adressé aux états généraux* (Paris, 1789).

24. *Nouvelle Biographie Générale*, Vol. 25 (1858), cols. 928-29.

25. *La Révolution de France prophétisée* . . . (Paris, 1791), 4.

26. Ibid., 5, 7ff.

27. Ibid., 20.

28. *Suite de "La Révolution de France prophétisée* . . . " (Paris, 1791), 80. Modern support for this approach is found in Gordon H. McNeil, "The Anti-Revolutionary Rousseau," *The American Historical Review*, LVIII (July 1953), 808–23.

29. *Suite de "La Révolution de France prophétisée. . . ."* 84–5.

30. Ibid., 86–87.

31. *La Révolution de France prophétisée. . .* , ii.

32. *Suite de "La Révolution de France prophétisée . . .* , 86.

33. *La Révolution de France prophétisée. . .* , 34.

34. Ibid., 37, 47ff.

35. Ibid., 276.

36. *L'Ami du Roi* (Royou), August 29, 1791, and *Journal de la Cour et de la Ville*, July 19, 1791, as cited in Jean Paul Bertaud, *Les Amis du Roi: Journaux et journalistes royalistes en France de 1789 à 1792* (Paris 1984), 62. Pursuing this theme even further, royalist journalists turned Louis XVI into a sacrificial victim. See Bertaud, 62–63.

37. *Ami du Roi* (Royou), prospectuses, September 1, 1790, February 5, 1791; William J. Murray, *The Right-Wing Press in the French Revolution: 1789–92* (Woodbridge, Eng., 1986), 253–54.

38. *Journal général de France*, July 21, 1791; Murray, *The Right-Wing Press in the French Revolution: 1789–92*, 254.

39. *Année littéraire*, no. 8, 1790, as cited in Murray, *The Right-Wing Press in the French Revolution: 1789–92*, 246–47.

40. Cited from Jean Paul Bertaud, *Les Amis du Roi: Journaux et journalistes royalistes en France de 1789 à 1792*, 69.

41. *Ami du Roi* (Montjoie), September 6, 1791 and March 1, 1792, as cited in Murray, *The Right-Wing Press in the French Revolution: 1789–92*, 255.

42. *Journal à deux liards*, VII, no. 5, in Murray, *The Right-Wing Press*, 255–56.

43. Ibid., 256.

44. Ibid., 257–59.

45. Cited from Bertaud, *Les Amis du Roi*, 73. Bertaud also quotes the July 17, 1791 issue of *L'Ami du Roi* in a similar sense, 71.

46. Pierre Escoube, "Un Versaillais méconnu: Sénac de Meilhan (1736–1803), *Revue de l'histoire de Versailles et des Yvelines*, 63 (1978), 17–19, 27; Pierre Escoube, *Sénac de Meilhan (1736–1803), De la France de Louis XV à l'Europe des émigrés, Suivi de: Du Gouvernement, des moeurs et des conditions en France, avant la Révolution (extraits)* (Paris, 1984), 200–201; Guy Pierre Marie Sénac de Monsembernard, *Sénac de Meilhan, 1736–1803* (Auch, 1969), 23–35, 72, 84–85, 96; Beik, *The French Revolution Seen from the Right*, 41.

47. Gabriel Sénac de Meilhan, *Des principes et des causes de la Révolution en France* (London, 1790), 10–13; Sénac de Monsembernard, *Sénac de Meilhan*, 98.

48. *Des principes et des causes de la Révolution en France*, 14.

49. Ibid., 19–21. For a modern interpretation of this controversy and its effects, see Dale K. Van Kley, *The Jansenists and the Expulsion of the Jesuits from France* (New Haven, 1975).

50. *Des principes et des causes de la Revolution*, 21.

51. Sénac de Monsembernard, *Sénac de Meilhan*, 100–115.

52. Gabriel Sénac de Meilhan, *Du gouvernement, des moeurs, et des conditions en France, avant la révolution; avec le caractère des principaux personnages du règne de Louis XVI* (Hamburg, 1795), 7.

53. d'Argenson served as foreign minister 1744–1747; Machault was controller general of finance 1745–1754 and secretary for the navy 1754–1757.

54. Sénac de Meilhan, *Du gouvernement, des moeurs, et des conditions en France, avant la révolution*, 93–94. Jacques Godechot, *La Contre-révolution. Doctrine et action (1789–1804)* (Paris, 1961), 45, says that Sénac de Meilhan may have been the first to identify the revolt of the nobles as an important cause of the Revolution. On Sénac's identification of an aristocratic resurgence, see also: Pierre Escoube, "Sénac de Meilhan, grand administrateur de l'Ancien Regime et juge de ses institutions," *Revue administrative*, 35 (1982), 138–39.

55. Sénac de Meilhan, *Du gouvernement*, 122–25.

56. Ibid., 128.

57. Ibid., 128–29.

58. Ibid., 130.

59. Ibid., 134.

60. *Des principes et des causes de la Révolution en France*, 34–35.

61. Ibid., 35.

62. Ibid., 26–27.

63. Although this seems a partial contradiction of Sénac's point mentioned in footnote 54—that the monarchs were not engaged enough in the political process.

64. *Du gouvernement*, 137–38.

65. *Des principes et des causes de la Révolution en France*, 28–29.

66. Ibid., 38–40.

67. Ibid., 45–46.

68. *Du gouvernement*, 180, 182.

69. Ibid., 59–60.

70. Ibid., 61–64.

71. Ibid., 64–65.

72. Ibid., 66–68.

73. Ibid., 72–74; see also *Du gouvernement*, 214–15.

74. *Des principes et des causes de la Révolution en France*, 78–79. Here, in 1790, is a very clear statement of the idea of the aristocratic resurgence. See footnote 54 for an earlier reference to it in the reign of Louis XV. Sénac said politics had been fashionable for the upper class, replacing the earlier quarrels between Jansenism and the Parlements, and those involving music. Such quarrels, he found, "had become the sole nourishment of ardent and light spirits, who experienced a perpetual need for agitation." *Des principes*, 79.

75. *Des principes*, 81.

76. Such management would have been incompatible with the elections that did take place.

77. *Du gouvernement*, 215–16. Here Sénac de Meilhan underestimated the goals of the representatives. Almost the same account is given in his *Portraits et caractères du XVIIIe siècle* (Paris, 1945), 65–6; see also *Des principes*, 92–9.

78. *Du gouvernement*, 184.

79. *Des principes*, 103, 105.

80. R. R. Palmer, *The Age of Democratic Revolution* (Princeton, 1959–1964), 2 vols.; Jacques Godechot, *Les Révolutions, 1770–1799* (Paris, 1963); Louis Gottschalk, *The Place of the American Revolution in the Causal Pattern of the French Revolution* (Easton, Pa., 1948).

81. For this question see: Northrup Frye, "The Problem of Spiritual Authority in the Nineteenth Century," in *Literary Views: Critical and Historical Essays*, Charles Carrol Camden, ed. Rice University Semicentennial Studies (Chicago, 1964), 145–58.

CHAPTER II

French Royalist Political Thought, 1789–1791

This chapter will provide an explanation of how French royalists sought to stand up to the challenge of the revolt during the early years of the French Revolution. To lead into this, I will provide a brief summary of absolutist thought earlier in the century.[1]

The eighteenth century advocates of royal absolutism began with Bishop Bossuet's argument of the divine right of kings, went on to defend absolutism by citing historical tradition (the argument from prescription),[2] and then sought to make use of the idea, as suggested by philosophes like Voltaire, that strong kings could best enact reforms in the face of the entrenched opposition of the aristocrats. By mid-century the earlier defenses of absolutism were being superseded by a utilitarian rationale. The problem with the new approach as a defense of monarchy was that if the monarch in fact did not institute reforms, then the rationale could lead to a call for another form of government.[3]

The marquis d'Argenson (1694–1757) is a case in point. His *Considérations sur le gouvernement ancien et présent de la France*, finished in 1737 but not published until 1764, called for "a powerful reforming absolutism, which would unhesitantly use the state's power to serve the general welfare, thus anchoring the monarchy firmly in the people."[4] Such a policy would involve the abolition of obstructive autonomous and feudal rights that stood in the path of reform. But the government of Louis XV did not follow his advice. After a discouraging and disillusioning period as minister of foreign affairs (1744–1747), the marquis concluded that the monarchy of Louis XV could not be the engine of reform and began to consider instead the virtues of a limited monarchy.[5]

The physiocrats are another example. They espoused what they called legal despotism. With the help of the physiocrats, the ruler was to find and apply the laws of nature. They "strongly believed in the regeneration of society through the enlightened action of one central authority."[6] But like d'Argenson before them, by the 1780s the physiocrats had become disillusioned with a monarchy that had failed to reform and had spurned the good advice of one of their number, Turgot. They turned toward political liberalism, which did not offer the short-cut that absolute monarchy had seemed to provide, but which seemed more practicable in France. So the end of the Old Regime saw the monarchy increasingly challenged by aristocratic and liberal ideas.

One of the last defenders of absolutism before the Revolution was Jacob Nicolas Moreau (1717–1803), a government propagandist who first attacked the philosophes[7] and then tried to use their ideas to defend the monarchy. In voluminous works published in the 1770s and 1780s,[8] he made a strenuous effort to defend enlightened traditionalism. He said that the ruler should be guided by natural law, which could be discovered through the use of reason. And he employed the philosophes' utilitarian rationale for power: the king must provide life, liberty, and defense of property. Furthermore, although the king had absolute legislative authority, he should use it only after seeking guidance from an enlightened body of advisors.[9]

Between 1787–1789, when royal authority was under increasingly heavy attack, Moreau desperately tried to find a way out. He attacked the aristocrats and sought to restore the old alliance of King and people against them. And he feared that the calling of the Estates-General might provide an opening wedge for democracy. Moreau also feared that Louis XVI in his weakness would abandon absolutism without a fight. So he argued that the King could not give up his position without the consent of the nation. As Paul Beik has pointed out, Moreau thus ended up in the ironic position of appealing to the forces of democracy to uphold the role of absolutism.[10]

Chaillon de Jonville, in his *Apologie de la constitution françoise* (1789), 2 vols., was one of the final defenders of absolutism before the French Revolution. He maintained that the constitution was good and should not undergo any basic changes. But he distinguished between the constitution and the administration, and admitted that the policies of some of the ministers were bad in part. Hence he did admit some wrongdoing, but, since the constitution and the King were good, all one had to do was to select good ministers.

Moreover, Chaillon de Jonville was cautious about making changes. In fact he anticipated Burke and the organic theory of history: "correct instead of destroying. There is even in the bad, when it is the work of time, a sort of harmony which supports the structure, and which is not always found in the good, when it is the sudden work of men. New operations are only good when they are placed in some fashion at the side of the constitution, and take effect by degrees and bring a long and slow perfection."[11]

So, as they saw the Revolution descend on them, royalists had to decide whether they could defend their cause by means of the divine right of kings argument, or by prescription, or by the organic theory of history. Furthermore they had to counter the notions of popular sovereignty and the contract theory of government.

Then they somehow had to defend the record of the Old Regime. Eventually they created a myth of the Old Regime as a time of peace, prosperity, and order. Whenever possible, the Right sought to turn the principles of the Revolution against the revolutionaries. It also had to combat the individualism inherent in the Revolution, arguing that society was more important than the individual.

Finally monarchists had a problem with Louis XVI, who did not behave the way they thought he should. At times he seemed to make common cause with the revolutionaries and go beyond the principles of June 23, 1789. Given his apparent weakness and vacillation, monarchists wondered whether they should invite foreign invasion and call for civil war. And, if they were fortunate enough to win, should they let bygones be bygones or seek to punish their political foes? In seeking to confront these issues, royalists began to forge the arguments that came to make up modern conservativism.

As the Right wrestled with these questions, it found itself divided into three groups. The royalists, the subjects of this study, aimed to preserve the absolute power of the King in the face of all challenges to his authority; the aristocrats, who had a taste of victory in their revolt against the monarch on the eve of the Revolution, wanted to increase and institutionalize their authority; and the anglophiles who wanted a representative constitutional monarchy in the English fashion. Their conflicts, which predated the Revolution, contributed to the success of the Revolution in 1789 and weakened any effort on the part of the Right to overthrow it.[12]

One of the early monarchist reactions to the French Revolution, probably written in the fall of 1789, was that of the abbé Jean Baptiste Du Voisin (1744–1813), canon of Laon, in his *La France chrétienne, juste et vraiment libre*. In this work Du Voisin said that any change that took place should be done gradually:

> Political governments are good, they are necessary only for the maintenance of peace; and peace can be affirmed only by the stability of governments. A constitution that could be freely changed every day is no better than the condition of the savages and the denial of government. It is worthless because this perpetual mutuality would multiply the subjects of discord, it would add a teeming and inexhaustible cause to the divisions always spring up again, to the miseries and the disorders that afflict scattered families, who do not live in society. If one could pass as one wished from one form of government to another, it would be to unite to divide, to torment oneself, to become mutually impoverished and destroy each other.[13]

So we have here, a year before Edmund Burke, the germ of the idea of the organic theory of history, one of the important contributions of royalists at this time to conservative political thought.

Christianity, Du Voisin argued, moderated authority and destroyed the chains of slavery, whereas despotism appeared wherever Christianity did not exist.[14] He then went on to defend, in the manner of Bossuet, the divine right of kings. Here he advanced the argument that "to recognize someone as sovereign, is to recognize him as the representative of the divinity, as the depository of an authority that comes from God and not properly from the multitude." The multitude could not be superior to itself; hence it could not bestow superiority over itself. God, alone, possessed this authority.[15]

Furthermore, God wanted order, and therefore he chose as his agents those necessary to establish peace and order. And God wanted us to obey them. It was God who received our promises of faithfulness to the sovereign, as if we had made them directly to Him. He also received the promises of the rulers, and He served as judge and arbiter between the ruler and the people.[16]

The king was powerful, but he was not despotic. He was limited not only by his responsibilities to God, but also by the constitution and by the fact that the people had agreed to accept the monarch in the first place. So there was no room for capriciousness. The interests of the subjects and the king were the same, and so the rule must be both monarchical and popular.[17]

The king, however, remained superior to and in fact was the chief of his people. He was not merely the first agent or the first minister. In other words, the king did not depend more on his subjects than they did on him. Du Voisin was convinced that God would not have bestowed the title of king if he did not intend him to be sovereign and independent.[18]

But since the king was not to be despotic, he should make use of the Estates-General. Du Voisin proposed a national council, made up of the most religious and judicious members of the Third Estate, the nobility, and the clergy; they would be elected freely but by a severely limited suffrage. Its job would be to receive complaints from throughout the kingdom, to send them, along with its recommendations, to the king, and to send a response to the interested parties. The important thing was that the king must leave free access of the people to him. "If the government and the ministry always arranges a free passage and an easy access near the throne for the complaints of the people and the weak, our Kings will only be our fathers, and justice and their goodness will continually increase our love."[19]

And Du Voisin thought that this arrangement would only work well if the aristocrats fostered communication between the parties, rather than working for their own interests. There is a suggestion here of the dangers of an aristocratic resurgence and an explicit defense of the age-old alliance between the king and the people.[20]

When it came to the rights of man, Du Voisin emphasized the restrictions on them. Man was born free, but was also born subject. He was subject to reason, the laws of God, nature, society, and the authority of parents, chiefs, and masters. At the same time he kept his natural rights. They included the right that liberty should not be restrained except by just laws, that innocent people should not be punished by any authority, and that the guilty could only be treated by legitimate authorities.[21]

Like Bossuet, the abbé Du Voisin came out strongly against freedom of conscience in matters of religion. Given the fact that France had established the true religion, which was closely tied to the state and the society, the introduction of other religions would trouble the public, religious, and political order, and introduce error, superstition, and illusion. He went on to say that true religion did not change at the pleasure of men. Since truth was not a human institution, it did not stop being true because of a change in human institutions. Therefore the Estates-General should protect true religion, not restrict it, and even less try to destroy it and start over again.[22] He also opposed freedom of the press on the grounds that the reading of impious and lascivious books had produced a great deal of evil. Freedom of the press, he thought, had done more to pervert France than it had to instruct and civilize it.[23]

Du Voisin is important for his suggestion of the organic theory of history, an idea that had little political resonance in 1789, but one that both conservatives and liberals would come to embrace after ten years of revolutionary upheaval and fifteen years of military despotism. But it is curious to see him trying to defend the divine right of kings, after the fashion of Bossuet, in 1789. It is significant that he placed limitations on the power of the king. Politically his most important idea was that the king had to reestablish his alliance with the people. To keep the lines of communication open there must be some kind of representative assembly. And he should not let the aristocrats get in the way.

The next royalist, the well-known abbé Augustin de Barruel (1741–1820), shared basic premises with Du Voisin. Both emphasized that there already were built-in limitations on the power of the king. Hence they said the current emphasis on representative government was beside the point. Both were deeply influenced by Bishop Bossuet; both sought to defend the divine right of kings and the importance of religion as a restraint on power and as a guide for the kingdom.

While best known for his theory that the French Revolution was the result of a conspiracy of philosophes, Freemasons, and Spiritualists,[24] Barruel also commented on the kind of government France should have. Beginning in January of 1789, he began to publish his first reactions to contemporary events in the *Journal ecclésiastique ou Bibliothèque raisonnée des sciences ecclésiastiques*. Later, in 1789, he issued them separately as *La patriote véridique, ou discours sur les vraies causes de la révolution actuelle*.[25]

Barruel began by insisting that the state had to be based on religion. He supported this assertion by arguing that a people without morality would always be unhappy and that those who let religion wither away were always working toward their own ruin. Religion would "prescribe just sacrifices to the rich, respect to the peoples, justice to the princes, obedience to subjects, integrity to magistrates, fidelity to ministers and administrators, charity, love, peace and concord to all. Religion, by retaining each in his duties, would make order reign everywhere and make the state happy by the virtue of all."[26]

Having established that foundation, Barruel then turned to a defense of absolute monarchy. Here he emphasized that France had a constitution and had an effective monarchy. The monarch, operating within his council, provided protection from outside enemies, and peace and order inside the kingdom. And, if old laws did not suffice, the prince and his council could issue new interpretations or make new laws. Moreover, the king directed each class in the performance of its duties to the state, provided equal protection under the law for all, and served as a source of unity.

Furthermore the king acted with the advice of his subjects. Usually this meant the king's council. But, when matters became more pressing, he convened all of the notables. And when the situation demanded it, he called together representatives of all of the nation, the Estates-General. Then all had a chance to register complaints, and propose ways and means to make changes. Finally, after he had been instructed by the nation, the king would issue new instructions.

The king could be distinguished from a despot because he issued laws protecting private property. All of the property of a citizen was sacred. The monarch could only tax that portion necessary for the needs of the nation. All the rest could be defended—if necessary in the courts. As long as one fulfilled his duties as a citizen, one had complete liberty. This meant that France had a constitution with definite guarantees.[27]

France had a satisfactory system. And the vast majority of the people loved the king and would be willing to fight, if need be, to defend him. They did not want any constitutional changes; they just wanted reform. They did not want to carry the burden of taxation, and they were upset at the exemptions of the rich. But they were misled by writers who told them that no law was valid without the approval of the Estates-General. Then people began to imagine that things would be better when lawyers ruled in the Estates-General, and it made the law. What one had to do was free the people and the writers of these illusions and make them realize that the overthrow of the constitution and the institution of alternatives would lead to anarchy and tyranny.[28]

The king made the laws, but they were holy, just, and all designed for the welfare of the nation. Law was something that a multitude could never make. Legislation should come from a small council, operating under a prince who had summoned the wisest advisers. Participation by a multitude would always lead to confusion and error because individuals saw only part of the picture. History taught that the most devoted republicans always demanded legislation from a single person, such as Solon at Athens and Lycurgus at Sparta. The so-called century of enlightenment saw liberty only in legislative supremacy. It did not realize that there was a vast difference between "the power of the people and the liberty of the people."[29]

Those who praised the English constitution to the skies should also describe the "rivers of blood it cost, the divisions it perpetuated, the inconceivable taxes it multiplied." They should let the French choose between kings that were revered and those that were subjected to humiliation, between a people who saw a fatherly figure on the throne and a people who always feared that a tyrant would be there.[30]

While Barruel admitted that there had been abuses under the French monarchy, he argued that the French constitution provided the best means to repair them. It was simple, active, and centralized; it had a prince whose sole desire was to love and be loved, and it followed nature because it established a father and his children. Instituting a new constitution, especially one that divided the country by providing a division of powers, would be the greatest abuse of all. Instead of blaming their constitution for their problems, the French should blame themselves. Their constitution had the sanction of fourteen hundred years behind it. Change would lead to terrible conflicts, and the results would be disastrous.[31]

In 1791, when the National Assembly was about to complete its task, Barruel assessed its work and defended his own principles again in *Question nationale sur l'autorité et sur les droits du peuple dans le gouvernement*. He began by admitting that he was prejudiced against the idea that "sovereignty resided essentially in the nation." "If I had to establish a principle of anarchy and disorder, a principle destructive of all government, it seems to me that this sovereignty of the people would present itself very naturally to my mind. I defy one to produce another that would favor insubordination more, that tends more directly to make it general, that subjects more strictly the law to all the caprices of the multitude, that consequently entails greater and more frequent disorders."[32]

On the basis of his study of constitutional history Barruel found no evidence for the idea that sovereignty rested in the nation. Appropriating the analysis of Rousseau for his own purposes, Barruel said that before the agreement to create a society, a state of complete independence and anarchy existed. After that people were busy deciding on the conditions by which they would lose their independence. At the time of the second contract, which established a government, they lost their autonomy and thereafter submitted themselves to the authority of a sovereign.[33] Barruel then went on to argue that this agreement was meant to endure with dynasties of hereditary leaders. If the pact was dissolved, people would then return to a condition of complete independence and anarchy. They then would not be sovereign, but would have to again recognize their need to call for a new sovereign.[34]

So the first part of his work was about the nature of authority, and he made it very clear he would not want 25 million sovereigns. Sovereignty he defined as the "duty to take care of and govern all for the welfare of all." The sovereign had the right to be obeyed because he was looking out for the general welfare. It was a logical absurdity, he thought, that everyone could handle these responsibilities for everyone else. All could not be sovereign. Furthermore, the more numerous the people, the more they needed to be led.[35]

Moreover, it was possible, in fact often desirable, that sovereignty reside in an individual. This was particularly the case in a large nation where the number of people with all their separate interests tended to increase the obstacles to achieving the general welfare.[36]

From a more fundamental point of view, Barruel used Bossuet's argument that no human pact created the duties and the rights of morality, and that it was twice as true that no human agreement established the duties and the rights of authority. Without the intervention of a superior being, there was no morality or authority, but only force and cunning.[37]

Following Bossuet, Barruel claimed God was the primordial cause of authority, the one who created the general order of society and the moral universe. This order led to the subordination of the family to its leader and the peoples to their kings. God, the author of society, was the author of authority. He made man as a social being, which led to the establishment of families, peoples, and nations, and set up authorities over each. Only God as creator could have made some to command and others to obey and thereby subordinated human will to human empires. So all authority derived from, and was subordinated to, God. And any time there was a modification in the form or the hands of authority, God alone made the change.[38]

Barruel turned next to the rights and the limitations of sovereignty. Again drawing on Bossuet, he said that first of all, the person of the sovereign was inviolable. Secondly, the power of the sovereign was absolute; he had all the power necessary to bring about the welfare of the people and to overcome all the obstacles that stood in the way. If this were not the case there would be situations in which the general welfare could not be achieved.[39] But the power of the sovereign was established for a fixed purpose, the welfare of the people. Sovereignty operated under fixed rules, both for the governor and the governed. The power of the sovereign was absolute, but it was not arbitrary. The sovereign could not do anything he wanted, as could a despot. The orders of a despot proceeded from caprice; "those of a true sovereign came from a will directed by constant rules towards the welfare of the people."[40]

Barruel went on to explain that the general rules that guided "the sovereign and the citizens towards the general interest were called *fundamental laws*." Some of them related to the very nature of government, determined its scope and could not be changed without changing the form of government. Others, which he described as secondary, were general rules laid down by the government "to direct the citizens towards the public interest." They could be changed according to time and circumstances.[41]

Barruel also argued that neither the people nor the sovereign alone could change the fundamental laws. They had made a contract: the people had agreed to obey as long as the fundamental laws were observed, and the sovereign had pledged to govern according to them. The contract could not be cancelled without an agreement of all of the parties. While this seems to be a concession to the times and seems to be operating in the spirit of the contract theory of government, Barruel went on to argue that every single individual, not just the majority, had to agree to changes, which would make change virtually impossible. Further he maintained that the only limitation on the sovereign's power was the fundamental laws. Hence he could do anything else he wanted to.[42]

Moreover, with his eye on the constitution-making of the National Assembly, Barruel said that in all good governments the secondary laws were approved by the executive power. Otherwise the leader would be in the untenable position of enforcing laws he found unjust. Or he would not enforce some laws. This would be undesirable because it would promote contempt for the law. Hence the leader must at least have a veto to block laws that he considered opposed to the public interest.[43]

Barruel continued his analysis by asserting that the essential objective of good government was not to do the will of the people, but to save them and make them happy. In fact they might be mistaken and might want something that would lead to disaster. So the leader must save the people in spite of themselves. Hence the will of the people did not determine what should be law, and thus it was not essential for good government that the people had legislative power.[44]

Appropriating Rousseau's rejection of representation,[45] Barruel maintained that representative government did not offer a way out either. The people could not really have representatives because the people did not have any definite opinions. They could have advocates or lawyers or would-be protectors, but not representatives in any meaningful sense. All they could do would be to elect deputies, who would make all the necessary decisions and who would not represent anyone but themselves.[46] Having cleared the ground for the sovereign, Barruel concluded with a discussion of his duties. "The sovereign is the minister of God; he is the second providence of his people. The great objective of this providence is the happiness of the peoples." It is his responsibility to promote it in all ways by his laws, just as the laws of God worked for the salvation of mankind.[47]

And, in a possible criticism of the Old Regime, Barruel argued that the happiness of individuals depended especially on the exercise of authority by the agents of the sovereign, who might promote it or abuse it. So the sovereign had to be especially diligent in selecting his officers. One must consider neither favor nor personal inclination, but limit oneself to those who would be useful to the people. And the sovereign had to supervise them carefully, punishing severely those who did wrong, and protecting and promoting all those who fulfilled their responsibilities.[48]

In his 1791 *Question nationale sur l'autorité et sur les doits du peuple dans le gouvernement*, he came out explicitly against the idea of popular sovereignty, which he considered a prescription for anarchy and disorder. The people did not know what they wanted; hence the sovereign had to look out for their welfare. Moreover, in establishing government originally the people lost all say and lost the right to make any changes, though it is unclear why this had to be so. Then he advanced the practical argument that one needed one person as sovereign in a large nation. Next he invoked divine sanctions: since God had participated in the original creation of authority he had to participate in any changes, though it is not clear how God would make his presence felt and how He would reveal His position. Barruel was content to point to the mystery and leave it untouched. Then he repeated that the sovereign was absolute, but not arbitrary; he was no despot. His final roadblock against change was the incredible argument that the sovereign and every single one of the people had to agree to any changes in the fundamental laws of the land. So, as the National Assembly was putting the final touches on the Constitution of 1791, Barruel sought to resist it with a combination of elitism, history (as he construed it), utilitarianism, and divine sanction.

The next royalist statement comes from Charles Alexandre de Calonne (1734–1802). During the French Revolution the former Controller General of Finance usually advocated a limited constitutional monarchy following the English pattern,[49] but in November 1790 the comte d'Artois called him to Turin. He then served as his chief adviser until the August 1792 invasion of France. At the beginning of this period of service, in November 1790, he published *De l'état de la France tel qu'il peut et qu'il doit être*, which falls within the absolutist camp.[50]

First of all he said the National Assembly had taken the wrong track from the beginning. While it could restore the monarchy to its former position, it had to completely change its approach. Calonne announced that as far as the government of the Old Regime was concerned, there was "almost nothing that it should change, correct or destroy."[51] This makes him even more of a champion of the old order than Barruel.

Whatever was done should receive the sanction of the King, but that assumed the King could exercise his will freely. At present he lacked the strength and the authority to have it valued and respected. He could only be free when the fundamental laws were observed.[52] So Calonne and the émigrés portrayed Louis XVI as a puppet in his professions of support for the Revolution and as one who must be freed.

The problem was that the National Assembly had usurped its authority. The Assembly was made up of people who constituted themselves legislators, when actually they were nothing more than agents who had the title of *députés des baillages*. They then presumed to issue decrees, when all they really could do was come up with proposals, which the King could accept or reject. Furthermore the King had to have the freedom and the initiative to propose measures better than those presented to him. So again, the Assembly was acting illegally.[53]

To govern a monarchy by republican principles would be to expose it to every calamity. A weak king would have to abandon authority to whomever could grasp it. Then others would fight for power. Eventually honest men would realize the cost of humiliating their king. Since the government was monarchical, one had to have the King enter into all the acts of administration.[54] On the other hand, the King with his full power would "calm all the passions, stop all the factionalism, set aside all the vengeance, dispel all the fears, and obliterate the memory of all the crimes committed against him."[55]

The final message was reserved for Louis XVI. The destiny of France could not be accomplished if the King neglected to use the modest amount of authority he had left and continued to go along with the designs of the revolutionaries. To surround oneself with those determined to destroy royal power could only result in the most disastrous consequences. Continuing on this course would eventually cause royalists to side with the republicans, and then the King would have lost his last hope.[56]

Calonne relied almost entirely on the argument of prescription: whatever existed under the Old Regime was made holy by the passage of time; it worked well then, and it would operate effectively again if given a chance. The King had final legislative authority, not members of a self-constituted National Assembly. Like Barruel, Calonne believed that any basic change would result in civil war and anarchy. The King, with the restoration of his full powers, could solve all the problems, although one wonders why he did not do so in the last years of the Old Regime. Finally, this message told the royalists in France and in exile not to believe Louis XVI when he said he was sanctioning aspects of the Revolution, and exhorted Louis XVI to stand up to the revolutionaries.

The next authors served as journalists in the right-wing press between 1789 and 1791. The most famous of them is Antoine Rivarol (1754–1801), who won the Berlin Academy prize in 1784 for his *Discours sur l'universalité de la langue française*, translated Dante, contributed occasionally to the *Mercure de France*, and won a place for himself by his wit in the literary salons of the Old Regime. As a revolutionary journalist, he wrote most of the articles in the *Journal politique national* (July 1789–May 1790), founded by the abbé Sabatier de Castres, and played a leading role in the *Actes des Apôtres*.[57]

Although usually counted among the absolutists, Francis Bertin has warned that Rivarol could change his position according to the circumstances, and that he was not always sincere in his professions. He stood by the royal declaration of June 23, condemned the emigration of the nobility, and labeled the upper nobility and the upper middle class enemies of the King. But he also defended the émigrés and spoke in favor of the aristocratic resurgence. Bertin charged that he changed his position as he changed his patrons.[58]

Rivarol did not have any illusions about Louis XVI. During the Old Regime he wrote of him: "As a king, he deserved his misfortunes because he did not know how to perform his craft; as a man, he did not deserve them. His virtues make him a stranger to his people."[59] But when the Revolution came along he made it clear in his columns in the *Journal politique national* that France needed a king, and that he would have preferred a revolution by the King. According to Rivarol, as soon as the King consulted the Estates-General, he lost his sovereignty. Then there was an interregnum. When the King lost respect, the people stopped obeying. And a revolution from on high should not have gone beyond the program of June 23, though later Rivarol accepted the ending of the privileges of the nobility and the clergy, and the idea of a two-house legislature, but only on condition that the King retain an absolute veto.[60]

Rivarol came out strongly against what he considered excessive innovation. He called the Declaration of Rights "a dangerous preface," which could lead to extreme revolution. He told the legislators that they should emphasize duties, as well as rights. Otherwise the people might raise the false hope that they could pass from civic to economic equality. He warned that legislative assemblies that made too many changes risked falling from power themselves. And, in what was to be a common accusation by the right wing, he charged that the deputies were impractical idealists, whose theories and metaphysical abstractions would lead to disaster.[61]

Rivarol believed that some kind of aristocracy would always exist and that the philosophes should explain why this was so, rather than vainly proposing alternatives. Rivarol and others on the extreme right, looking back to the idea of *noblesse oblige* and to the responsibilities of a corporate society, thought that there were ties linking the "haves" and the "have nots," and that the poor instinctively depended on the rich. Hence the poor would not profit from the distress of the rich; rather all would fall into ruin. But if inequality was bound to exist, it had to be made palatable. So the extreme right held up the Church as an institution that not only supported absolutism, but also offered comfort and consolation for all who occupied an inferior place.[62]

The *Journal politique national*, written by a master stylist who tried to defend the old order during a time in which most political currents were running strongly in favor of liberalism, encountered strong opposition. But Rivarol was undaunted. He characterized his opponents as "the enemies of peace, royal authority, public happiness and common sense." And Rivarol had the satisfaction of hearing from Edmund Burke that his articles eventually would be placed beside Tacitus' *Annals*.[63]

Although the *Journal politique national* ran until May of 1790, Rivarol also participated in Jean Gabriel Peltier's *Actes des Apôtres* (November 1789–October 1791). Here there were fifteen to twenty contributors or "apostles," who did not all agree politically. Furthermore only a few of the articles can be identified with Rivarol. Nevertheless he played a major role in drawing up the paper. If the *Journal politique national* was partisan and pointed, the *Actes des Apôtres* was razor-sharp and vicious. Through wit and satire it attacked the individuals and the institutions of the Revolution without mercy. It made fun of real or imagined physical weakness, marital trouble, and political failure, focusing on the pornographic and scatological aspects where possible. All was fair in the effort to cut down the revolutionaries.[64]

In its columns nothing was spared, including the royal family. Louis XVI was described as "the watchmaker king" and the supposed amorous intrigues of Marie Antoinette were related. But it saved most of its fire, of course, for the Revolution. The National Assembly represented anarchy and chaos. Its decisions were only those of a minority faction, which had absolutely no importance. One could only have contempt for the "filthy riding school," which was "always full of manure." As a result, the *Actes des Apôtres* called for the worst possible punishments for the revolutionaries: "One must . . . chase out all the demagogues, hand over Charles Lameth, Barnave Duport, Robespierre, the bishop of Autun, Mirabeau (the older), Chapelier . . . to the most severe justice and feast on the spectacle of seeing them all undergo the same fate that we make the toads in the countryside undergo, hanging them up on hooks at the end of poles over the ruins of the Bastille and making them die by inches."[65]

The next journalist to tackle the Revolution was Pierre Barnabe Farmian de Rozoi (1742 or 1743–1792), editor of the *Gazette de Paris* (October 1, 1789–August 10, 1792). He failed to succeed as a writer under the Old Regime, but he made his mark with this paper. De Rozoi, who wrote most of the articles himself, moved to a counter-revolutionary position gradually. From March 1790, however, until his execution on August 25, 1792, he came out strongly and consistently for the monarchy.

De Rozoi attacked the Revolution as violently as Rivarol and the *Actes des Apôtres*, although he lacked their style and verve. He said the National Assembly was illegal, Necker the enemy of France, and he tore Mirabeau, Robespierre, and Desmoulins to shreds. For de Rozoi "the Revolution was a series of revolts: of pride against nature, of irreligion against faith, of the republican spirit against the monarchy, of crime against justice, of indecency against morality, of subjects against their king." He called for the complete restoration of the Old Regime, and attacked constitutional monarchists as much as republicans.[66]

The *Gazette de Paris* had a fairly large circulation. In January of 1791, it published 4,000 copies, though its circulation later dropped to 2,900 in May of 1792, and declined further during that summer. It speaks to the relative freedom of the press in the first years of the Revolution that a paper that not only attacked the Revolution but supported the counter-revolution was able to keep publishing until the fall of Louis XVI.[67]

Because his paper published to the very end, because de Rozoi was martyred for his faith, and because he opposed the Revolution in every way, de Rozoi stands as a champion of the counter-revolution par excellence. What he wanted to do was restore the glory of France's past. To this end he offered his readers a daily challenge to follow him on a new crusade.[68]

His defense of the French monarchy was perhaps most clearly stated in a article called "Principles of the Monarchy," which appeared on June 4, 1790. He began with a quotation: "Liberty and Monarchy are sisters: one should not, one could not separate them. The *happiness* and the security of the People depend on their inviolable concurrence."[69] He went on to advance a defense based on tradition. As recognized by constitutional law, France was a monarchy. One had to beware of new principles that destroyed the heritage of 1,400 years and actually created a republic, while still calling it a monarchy.

The best historians, he said, agreed that Hugh Capet was not summoned to power by an assembly of the nation, but assumed power as liege lord over the other lords and vassals. Since that time the power of the kings was based on the sword and on their genius, and it was not divided or shared with anyone. The people concurred in the government, but that was all. He then quoted Chancellor d'Aguesseu: "they concur only to *serve as instruments* to the one who is naturally the master of all men, God, from whom alone the person who mounts the throne receives all his authority."[70]

According to de Rozoi, there were two prerequisites for a society: the king, who was the source of obedience, and the pope, the source of faith. After the ending of hereditary nobility and titles on June 19, 1790, his paper was full of attacks on the Jacobins and the Protestants, who threatened the two sources of authority and therefore had to be eliminated. This became his rallying call for the counter-revolution. By September of 1791, he had decided that the Jacobins were responsible for all the uprisings that were destroying France.[71]

As de Rozoi reviewed the past year on January 1, 1791, he described France as a scene of desolation. Many unfortunate people had died as a result of violence, misery, and famine. Others had been forced to flee because of "the terror, the tortures, the slander, and the outrages" they had encountered. In fact he declared that by death and by flight France had lost more people in the last year than after the Battle of Poitiers. He closed his New Year's analysis by praying that the King would find the strength to lead his people back to the paths of goodness, order, and peace.[72]

De Rozoi was a man of fiery opinions, but he also was a man of action. He condemned the Civil Constitution of the Clergy, defended refractory priests, let them write in his paper, and collected gifts for them. On April 13, 1790, after the nationalization of the King's lands, he launched a subscription to help buy them back. Following the suppression of pensions for widows of army officers, he raised money for them. After the failure of the flight to Varennes in June of 1791, de Rozoi proposed that true royalists offer to serve as hostages for the King. About 900 offered to do so. He encouraged emigration and collected funds for émigrés. These efforts, as well as the "vengeance list" he compiled in 1792, involved him implicitly in the organization of the counter-revolution. He rejoiced at the allied invasion in the summer of 1792, though he thought the Brunswick Manifesto, which may have sealed the King's fate, was not strong enough![73]

The *Gazette de France* reflected its editor. It lacked effective analysis, was short on solid reporting, and was deprived of the levity of satire, but it was fed by the fertile imagination of its editor and by the many contributions of its subscribers. It succeeded above all because of its fiery style, its dedication, and its call to action.[74]

One of the most influential right-wing journalists was the abbé Thomas Marie Royou (1743–June 22, 1792), priest and professor for over twenty years at the College Louis-le-Grand, who collaborated on two newspapers before the Revolution, the *Journal de Monsieur*, and the *Année litteraire*, edited by his brother-in-law, Elie Fréron. In May of 1790, the directors of the *Année litteraire* decided to establish a new journal, *L'Ami du Roi*, which began publication on June 1. But a quarrel broke out among the editors, and Royou, claiming to be the true successor of Fréron, left his colleagues and began his own *L'Ami du Roi* (September 1, 1790–May 4, 1792).

Royou's *L'Ami du Roi* had a circulation of 5,000 in 1791, and 4,000 in 1792, larger than that of the *Gazette de Paris*. Royou carried on Fréron's assault on the philosophes. He tried to frighten the bourgeoisie and make it turn away from the Revolution, which he said would lead it to financial and political disorder. He also appealed to the mass of the people, whom he said were being used by political factions to advance their own interests. In 1791, Royou took his stand on the royal reform program of June 23, 1789; by 1792, he had stepped back to demand the return of all of the Old Regime.[75]

Shortly after he started his own paper in September of 1790, Royou argued that members of the National Assembly, who had been sent simply as commissioners or deputies to enact laws that the nation had indicated, had no power to draw up a constitution on their own. He asked what right a few men had to tell a whole nation to accept a constitution it had not examined and had no chance to approve. Popular sovereignty, which the Assembly had gratuitously bestowed on the nation, was an illusion. Actually the people only had the shadow of liberty and sovereignty. They were free during the elections for the Estates-General; thereafter they became slaves. "All their authority was reduced to the right to name their tyrants."[76]

The next spring Royou launched a more fundamental attack on the work of the National Assembly in two long articles in *L'Ami du Roi*.[77] Starting out with Rousseau, he said that individuals in a state of nature, realizing the inadequacy of their abilities, had surrendered all their rights to society as a whole. This surrender was "absolute, unlimited, irrevocable, and perpetual." Thenceforth individual interests had to suffer if necessary for the welfare of all. Otherwise the contract would be broken and anarchy would ensue, which would be much worse than any individual injury that might occur.

Soon after society was formed, the people realized that they were unable to govern themselves. They understood that the diversity of personalities, the conflict of interests and of passions, and the ignorance of most of the members would soon lead to the anarchy that had prevailed in the state of nature. So society had to divest itself of the authority it had acquired and place it in the hands to rulers. And, given the proven failure of society to rule, this cessation of power also had to be complete and for all time. If this were not the case, society would again disintegrate into anarchy.

"What," Royou asked rhetorically, "would be the stability of a government delivered to the caprices of an ignorant and passionate multitude, which did not know its true friends or its true interests, which always let itself be easily seduced by the attraction of novelties, the sumptuous promises of charlatans, the illusion of eventual happiness, by the gold of the ambitious, by the hope of a better fate in a revolution?" The answer would be chaos. And, since there always were plenty of ambitious rascals who held out false promises, society must resist their siren songs.

So the notion of popular sovereignty was a myth. Royou's rendition of Rousseau was that people possessed sovereignty only for a moment and only to give it up forever. While the origin of power came from the people, they were incapable of exercising it. Hence they should not try to seize it again. Since the people lacked knowledge of laws and constitutions that would promote their welfare, they could never change their form of government.

Then Royou began to build his case on the basis of Bossuet. He said that people, realizing their incapacities, could confer authority on any legitimate form of government they chose, extending or restricting power as most appropriate. Then the Supreme Being stamped whatever choice they made with the seal of His authority. So authority came both from people and from God. Once that choice had been made and confirmed by God, the authorities were invested with their power and thereafter ruled in the name of God. The people then could not dispossess their rulers without revolting against God himself.[78]

Those who were most enlightened put themselves under the control of one person. They understood that they would be safer under one than under a powerful assembly, which would be much more likely to enslave them.[79] Fearing the intrigues of political factions, they wanted to link themselves forever to rulers who would protect their rights, defend their property, and ensure their welfare. So they chose a family and placed all their hopes and confidence in it.[80]

Among the nations that abdicated their sovereignty forever to a single person, Royou went on, were the French people. They had experienced the difficulties caused by factions and by senates, and they had learned about civil wars brought about by tribunes and decemvirs. To avoid these calamities they chose one leader, and they did not want to be considered as subjects, but only as children of a hereditary leader. Furthermore, they unanimously recognized in their primary assemblies in 1788 and 1789 that authority was hereditary and inviolable in France, affirmed it in all their cahiers, and ordered their deputies, under oath, to proclaim it publicly. By these means the nation declared that it would always consider the king sacred and inviolable, and the throne hereditary. The clear implication then was that any changes made after the Estates-General convened violated French experience, law, and tradition, and were in direct opposition to the expressed wishes of the French people.[81]

In *Année litteraire* and *L'Ami du Roi*, Royou had already argued that imperfections in society could not be avoided; any attempt to improve them would be futile. One had to put up with bad administration because all men were sinful, because any attempts to change it would produce greater problems, and any change in the form of government would cause chaos. Stability and order, even an order based on some injustice, were vastly superior to freedom and the anarchy associated with it. Hence reason, pride, and individuality had to bow silently before law and authority.[82]

Royou used the example of the inability of the authorities to put down a food riot at Douai (Dord) in the spring of 1791 to drive home his point:

> such is what must result from a government that is not based on obedience and subordination. It was falsely thought that to ensure the success of the Revolution all that was necessary was to free the people from every restraint; and by that infernal policy they have not established liberty, but have made despotism necessary. This division of powers established by the Constitution is the annihilation of all powers, whilst the departments, districts, and municipalities dispute among themselves, get in each other's way, and hold each in check, the field is always left free for the sedition-mongers and the factions.

There will never be other than a single, absolute, and arbitrary authority that can put an end to anarchy; thus for not having been willing to put up with the gentle and paternal rule of our kings, we will fall under the yoke of tyrants, and license will have led us to servitude.[83]

Royou emphasized that the laws had to be obeyed, rather than that they had to be just. And he thought the community as a whole more important than individuals. Though some individuals might endure harm, that was better than the greater harm of upsetting public order. Furthermore it was preferable for one person to undergo wrong if the society as a whole was still safe, than for one criminal to escape punishment and subject the community to further wrongdoing. He believed that one of the greatest virtues of the Old Regime was its police, who provided protection for all citizens and for their property. He was upset that the National Assembly disregarded the criminal code of the Old Regime, which he thought one of its most enlightened measures. And he was skeptical of the new legal system of the Assembly, saying that it might introduce new laws, but would have great trouble getting them followed.

The executive authority of the Old Regime had worked, Royou and others on the Right thought, because it had all been vested in the king. The lawlessness of the French Revolution came from taking authority from him. One had to have strong executive authority, not only to maintain law and order, but also to keep the kingdom united; otherwise provinces would break off and establish autonomous republics. Decentralization, attempted by the National Assembly, was completely irresponsible. And letting people elect their own local officials would lead to anarchy and corruption. So the Revolution was destroying law and order, and undermining national unity.[84]

Like Rivarol, Royou and other rightists took aim at the revolutionary concept of equality. While the abolition of nobility might directly affect only a relatively small proportion of the population, they thought the equalizing frenzy might eventually affect all. Rightists claimed that revolutionaries actually became less concerned with equality when they had achieved the level they wanted. Royou believed that while equality was attractive in theory, it was unworkable in practice. Some were created to lead and others to follow. Hence those who argued against these distinctions were trying to undermine the natural order of society.[85]

Underlying the Right's discussion of sovereignty, authority, law, and equality was its attitude toward the people, who had thrown off their usual tranquility and destroyed a monarchy 1,400 years old. And the people showed no signs of returning to their previously assigned place. How could the beast carry on without the rider?

All of the Right believed that the people did not know their best interests. Hence government might be for the people, but it could not be by them. Rivarol said the people were tranquil only when they were digesting. One erred in taking food away from them and in letting them rule. François Louis Suleau in the

Journal de M. Suleau agreed and said that if they were fed they would not want to govern themselves.[86]

Those on the Right who had no clerical ties were completely contemptuous of the people. Rivarol said they staggered toward freedom by cutting across the rights of others. They had no understanding and were little better than beasts. Suleau considered them scum, who would return to their usual place in society as soon as others stopped provoking them.

Those who had church ties, such as the abbé Royou, did not want to condemn them as strongly so as to avoid a slur on the order God had created. They portrayed them as weak, simple people who were easily misled by others. They had been led astray by Jacobins and Protestants into thinking they were oppressed and did not realize that freedom would lead to their own destruction, that equality could not exist. Lacking the guidance of the Church and the authority of the King, they had fallen into evil hands.

Education, the Right believed, would not work. One could not hope to reach the masses through reason because they were unreasonable. They were ignorant and the Right hoped they would remain that way. Monarchists at this time had not yet learned that ultimately they might count on the support of the people. So they shut their eyes and hoped the nightmare would go away.[87]

In spite of the abbé Royou's strong opposition to the French Revolution, unlike other rightists he saw little chance of success for a counter-revolution and little likelihood of intervention by outside powers. The united *L'Ami du Roi* first stated this position on July 30, 1790:

> In a word, despite the peaceful views of the Assembly, the writers and the incendiary clubs have done everything necessary . . . to raise up against us all the European powers; but we see nothing that indicates that they are thinking of profiting by our weakness. These powers, especially England and Prussia, are too informed to want, by a declaration of war, to put an end to the cruel divisions that rend the bosom of that unfortunate country, much more deeply than any enemy could do.[88]

Royou expanded on the theme of popular revolution and civil war in the first issue of his own newspaper, September 1, 1790. After observing that one could not establish a stable constitution on a foundation of violence and terror, and that good legislation could never come from popular uprisings, he argued that the people, who were easily misguided, always needed an authority to contain them. Democracy, he thought, was the worst form of government, especially for a large country like France. It produced sedition, discord, and raised false hopes. A wise ruler did not try to provide the best possible legislation, but the best the people could possibly use. The people did not have the capacity to treat the affairs of state seriously. The thing to fear was that, after destroying all the worthwhile principles and institutions, the people would end up hating all authority and lead the nation into civil war. While Royou recognized that abuses called for reforms, he said that "to destroy instead of reforming, is to heal a sick person by killing him."

Man freed from the checks of religion and law became a ferocious animal. Fanaticism took possession of him and made him treat cruelty as an amusement. And the worst thing about fanatics was that they plunged themselves into excesses without a second thought and without remorse.[89]

But in conclusion once again he ruled out a counter-revolution. Those who advocated it were insane and should be committed. Instead he called for time, for experience to bring an understanding of the situation. History, however, did not offer comfort. Past experience taught that "anarchy never ceded to laws, but to force; and that the despotism of all always gave way to the despotism of one."[90]

As problems began to develop in the French Revolution, the Right began to extol the beauties of the Old Regime. In October of 1790 Christophe Félix Montjoie, in his version of *L'Ami du Roi*, said that the Old Regime was definitely preferable to the new one. And on January 29, 1791, his competitor, the abbé Royou, reported that the people had begun to say that they would overthrow the Revolution and restore the Old Regime.

This became a frequently stated position in the right-wing press by 1791. On June 18th, Royou painted an idyllic picture of the Old Regime: there was peace, law, full employment, and no starvation. Bread shortages existed only under the Revolution. The poor had benefited most of all. It was only after the Revolution began that they started to suffer. Workers had not been sent to the Bastille and had not been affected by the *lettres de cachet*. Since they possessed nothing, the government could take nothing from them. In fact, Royou argued that "poverty is the surest guarantee of liberty."[91]

While Rouyou's tone usually sought to provide convincing rationalizations, Gautier de Syonnet relied on the power of emotion. Jacques Louis Gautier de Syonnet's *Journal de la Cour et de la Ville*, popularly known as *le Petit Gautier* (September 16, 1789–August 10, 1792), may have sold more papers than any other on the far Right, perhaps as many as 10,000. While originally sympathetic to the Revolution, by May of 1790, it had become a spokesman for the opposition. Like Royou's *L'Ami du Roi* it thought the Estates-General had no right to create a new constitution. All one had to do was enforce the existing constitution and abolish a few abuses. But there should be no concessions beyond the royal declaration of June 23, 1789.[92]

This journal became fairly hysterical at the news of the death of Mirabeau on April 2, 1791. It reported that he had been poisoned, said he was an extraordinary man, and that without him France was lost. Since he was the only one who could save France, "his death was a calamity," a turning-point in the Revolution. The problem was the French did not know how to avenge him. The King, who had been handed over to his enemies, could do nothing. As a result the duc d'Orléans and the Jacobins would triumph.[93]

Then the flight to Varennes provoked a veritable frenzy in the press. Gautier de Syonnet in the *Journal de la Cour et de la Ville* found the whole thing overwhelming:

> The most disastrous news has come one after the other with such frightful speed! Fear, hope, all the most painful feelings have tortured us in turn and, far from seeing an end to our troubles, the future indicates only signs of the most fearful storm.
>
> While we were giving ourselves up yesterday to transports of an imprudent joy, while we delighted in portraying the touching moment when the King would press his faithful subjects in his arms, against his heart; well, in this very moment, the monarch is returning in the chains that he had vainly tried to break. . . .[94]

But the most reasoned and constructive royalist response to the flight came in two long articles from the abbé Royou, who tried to justify it and to vindicate the King. Royou depicted Louis XVI as an innocent prisoner, who had been held against his will. Naturally he sought his freedom.

And he asked what right the nation had to establish its liberty on the slavery of its king. Was he to be the only exemption from the natural rights enumerated in the constitution? And, if property was the guarantee of liberty, as the Declaration of Rights assumed, why should the King be stripped of his property? Did he not have the same right as anyone else to seek his safety and that of his family? Given the danger he faced, flight was a necessity.

His enemies said he sought the frontiers to rally the émigrés and the foreign princes so he could return to France and impose despotism. That was a lie. He had always shown himself concerned only with the welfare of his subjects, no matter what personal sacrifices he had to make. He had always wanted only to be the father and the friend of his people. Furthermore, it was unreasonable to expect that foreign powers would be indifferent to what was happening in France. Naturally they wanted to protect their peoples from the epidemic of revolution, especially since the revolutionaries were trying to spread their contagion abroad. So if a foreign alliance formed against France, France had caused it. Furthermore the foreigners would be aided by the many Frenchmen who were suffering from the Revolution. So France faced a terrible foreign and civil war.

In this critical situation the King, who could not prevent foreign invasion while in captivity and whose captors opposed peace, decided to place himself between the French and the powerful nations who threatened them. Hence he left for Montmédy to work as an unfettered peacemaker. Given his objectives, his departure should have been received with "transports of love and thanksgiving."

What, he asked, would have happened had Louis XVI reached Montmédy? In that case, buttressed by his supporters, he would have been able to negotiate with the revolutionary government. And the people would have realized the advantages of accepting a new constitution, which would not only have eliminated the abuses of the Old Regime but the even greater ones of the current constitution. The result would have been a constitution that was truly national because it was based on the freedom of all the contracting parties. Then France would have enjoyed domestic tranquility, order, unity, prosperity, and peace with its neighbors.

Had the King not tried to regain his independence, foreign powers would have invaded, and brought death and destruction in their wake. And civil war would have broken out in France. Maybe the Revolution would have won, but it would have produced rivers of blood and erected its constitution on a pile of ruins and corpses. So the arrest of the King actually was a terrible calamity.

Royou also responded to the charge that the King, in violating his sacred promises to uphold the new order, had broken the ties that held him to the people; hence he was no longer fit to reign. Royou found it strange that men who had violated their oaths of loyalty and rebelled against the King should be so exigent. Moreover a promise was valid only if it were freely obtained—not the case here. His flight proved his captivity. The only people who were guilty of wrongdoing were those who undermined his freedom and held him by violence. The new constitution said that the sanction of the King was an indispensable part of the law-making process. Without it all decrees were null and void. Nevertheless the revolutionaries had broken their own constitution by trying to force his agreement. And now, after the flight to Varennes, they were violating it again by saying that the King's sanction was no longer necessary and that laws could be executed without it.

Royou then took up the question of the inviolability of the King, which was proclaimed in the constitution. This was done to provide him with sufficient power, authority, and prestige to enforce the law. Now, in attacking that inviolability, the revolutionaries were attacking their own constitution and undermining the authority of the one person who could carry out the principles of liberty, equality, and fraternity.

Royou concluded by calling on the French to return power to the King. Without it there would be no domestic peace, but only discord, no true freedom, but only license and anarchy. To make this authority effective, the King had to be truly free; otherwise there would be "no constitution, no laws, no order, no tranquility."[95]

Royou thus attempted to use the principles proclaimed by the Revolution against the revolutionaries themselves. As far as the charge that Louis XVI was seeking to ally with foreign powers against France was concerned, Royou practiced the stout denial, though evidence was accumulating to the contrary. And it was an important point, though not popular at the time, that foreigners considered the Revolution a threat, especially when the French sought to export its ideas. It is not clear, however, that Louis XVI's new constitution would have had much appeal, particularly when Royou failed to spell out what it would be like. Finally, Royou's analysis carries the implicit threat that unless Louis XVI was freed, France would be subjected to invasion and civil war. This was the threat of the Brunswick Manifesto of 1792, which linked Louis XVI irrevocably with France's national enemies and thereby led to his overthrow.

The marquis of Bouillé, in his letter to the National Assembly after the failure of the flight to Varennes, took much the same line. Depicting Louis XVI's intended role as that of a mediator between France and the foreign powers, he again posed the threat: "the princes of Europe who are menaced by the monster you have given birth to, plan to attack you." Bouillé went on to argue that France was defenseless and would be subjected to a terrible punishment. While seeking to assume all the responsibility for what had happened himself, he warned that if even a hair on Louis XVI's head was disturbed he would lead in the foreign armies, France would be devastated, and Paris leveled.[96] Thus the pattern for Brunswick was set.

But it was left to Count Emmanuel Louis d'Antraigues (1754–1812), a leader of the counter-revolution, to prove conclusively that the failure of the flight had not chastened the extreme right, but only made it more intransigent. *Point d'accommodement*, the title of his pamphlet, summer of 1791, became the rallying cry of the royalists, who adopted his program in their drive for power in 1792. He tried to stiffen the resolve of Louis XVI by arguing that the king could not make any changes in the traditional constitution himself. That could happen only if the three orders, assembled in their bailiwicks, requested specific changes, which the king could approve. In the meantime, the king could not give up any of his powers, but had to transmit them intact to his successors. Any king who failed to do so automatically forfeited his right to the crown and had to make way for his successor. The people had to die for the throne, and the king had to die for the monarchy. All he could do, and what he had to do, was to eliminate abuses.

Antraigues also linked the defense of the rights of the king of France with those of all kings. If the sovereigns of Europe consented to the loss of power by the king of France, they therefore forfeited the right to defend their own powers. So the nations had to restore Louis XVI to all of the authority he had enjoyed before the Estates-General of 1789.

Finally, Antraigues held out no hope for a general amnesty following the restoration of the monarchy. Punishment awaited those who had forced the royal family to move to Paris in October of 1789, who prevented their escape in 1791, and who had subverted the constitution by turning the Estates-General into the National Assembly.[97]

Under the challenge of the French Revolution, French royalists thus continued and developed the arguments for royal power that originated earlier in the eighteenth century. Obsessed with the need for order during a time of revolutional upheaval, they clung to the argument from prescription, which said the French people had abandoned any power they possessed and had given it forever to their kings.

They also resurrected the divine right of kings rationale, According to this argument authority was sacred; it came from God, not from the people, and only God could sanction any change. Christianity played an indispensable role in society: it was a prerequisite both for order and for virtue.

Royalists put the emphasis on the needs of the community, rather than on individuals. The great virtue of kings was they had provided order and protection, and had defended the rights of private property. So royalists advanced a utilitarian argument to defend their position. Kings ruled to promote the welfare of the people; hence they had to be strong to achieve this objective.

To avoid upsetting the apple cart, any change should come gradually. Otherwise impractical idealists, such as the revolutionaries, would raise false expectations that would lead to political disaster. To further defend their position, royalists created a myth of the Old Regime, where there was peace and plenty for all.

In addition to buttressing their own position, royalists attacked the views of their opponents. Since royalists subscribed to the organic theory of history and since English institutions were a source of inspiration to revolutionaries, they depicted England as a land of political division, bloodshed, tyranny, and high taxation.

They were careful to argue that while French kings were absolute, they were not despots. The king was limited by God, by the traditional constitution, and by the needs of the people. And he had to keep the political channels open. What people had to realize was that the overthrow of the constitution would lead to anarchy and to tyranny. And separation of power between national and local governments would speed the way to political disaster.

Royalists attacked the ideas of popular sovereignty and the contract theory of government because they maintained that the people were incapable of governing. And rightists claimed that those who would abolish inequality would undermine the natural order of society. Inequality would continue to exist and the "have nots" would continue to depend on the "haves."

Besides engaging in theoretical arguments, many of them were ready to take action against their foes, though the inactivity and the apparent political vacillation of Louis XVI made it difficult for them to find a leader. Most rightists supported counter-revolution. While the French Revolution became an international crusade, counter-revolution became one too, with royalists linking the fate of monarchy in other countries to that in France. The remarkable thing about the royalists was that they made no bones about their intention to crush their foes when they returned to power. So both ends of the political spectrum established a pattern of intolerance, threats, retribution, violence, and civil and international war.

NOTES

An earlier version of this chapter appeared as "French Absolutist Political Thought, 1789–1791," in *Proceedings of the Consortium on Revolutionary Europe* 16 (1986), 21–34.

1. For a fuller account of royalist thought before the Revolution, see Paul H. Beik, *The French Revolution Seen from the Right: Social Theories in Motion, 1789–1799* (Philadelphia, 1956), 3–13.

2. abbé Jean Baptiste Dubos (1670–1742), *Histoire critique de l'établissement de la monarchie française* (1734).

3. Peter Gay, *Voltaire's Politics: The Poet as Realist* (Princeton, 1959), 333; T. Bestermann, "Voltaire, Absolute Monarchy and the Enlightened Monarch, *Studies on Voltaire and the Eighteenth Century* 32 (1965), 19–21.

4. Beik, *The French Revolution Seen from the Right*, 6.

5. Franz Neumann, *The Democratic and the Authoritarian State* (Glencoe, Ill., 1957), 110–11; Henri Sée, *L'Évolution de la pensée politique en France au XVIIIe siècle* (Paris, 1925), 93, 102; Gerald J. Cavanaugh, "Vauban, d'Argenson, Turgot: From Absolutism to Constitutionalism in Eighteenth-century France," Unpublished dissertation (New York, 1967), 165.

6. Leo Gershoy, *The French Revolution and Napoleon* (New York, 1933, 1964), 71.

7. In his *Nouveau Mémoires pour servir à l'histoire des Cacouacs* (1757), he said that the philosophes lived in tents, believed in anarchy, advocated moral relativism to the point of nihilism, and agreed among themselves only when their object was destruction.

8. *Leçons de morale, de politique et de droit publique, puisées dans l'histoire de notre monarchie* (1773); *Les devoirs du prince reduits à un seul principe, ou Discours sur la justice, dedié au Roi* (1775); *Principes de morale, de politique et de droit public* (1777–1789), 21 vols.; *Essai sur les bornes des connaissances humaines* (1784); *Variétés morales et philosophiques* (1785), 2 vols.; *Exposé historique des administrations populaires, aux plus anciennes époques de notre monarchie* (1789); *Maximes fondamentales du gouvernement françois* (1789); *Exposition et défense de notre constitution monarchique françoise* (1789), 2 vols.

9. Beik, *The French Revolution Seen from the Right*, 9.

10. Ibid., 10–11.

11. Chaillon de Jonville, *Apologie de la constitution françoise; ou États républicains et monarchiques, comparés dans les Histoires de Rome et de France* I (1789), 161.

12. William J. Murray, *The Right-Wing Press in the French Revolution: 1789–92* (Woodbridge, Eng., 1986), 168.

13. [Jean Baptiste Du Voisin] *La France chrétienne, juste et vraiment libre* (n.p., 1789), 158–59.

14. Ibid., 152.

15. Ibid., 153. For the idea that the authority of kings came from God, see Jacques Benigne Bossuet, *Politique tirée des propres paroles de l'Écriture sainte*, Édition critique avec introduction et notes par Jacques Le Brun (Geneva, 1967), 44, 46, 64–65, 271–72.

16. Du Voisin, *La France chrétienne*, 154. On the necessity to obey kings, who were God's agents to promote order, and on God as the supreme arbiter, see Bossuet, *Politique tirée des propres paroles de l'Écriture sainte*, 69, 287, 289, 290.

17. Du Voisin, *La France chrétienne*, 211, 212; Bossuet, *Politique tirée des propres paroles*, 291–93.

18. Du Voisin, *La France chrétienne*, 212–13.

19. Ibid., 151–52. This is related to R. R. Palmer's argument that the failure of the Old Regime was a failure of public relations. See *The Age of Democratic Revolution, A Political History of Europe and America, 1760–1800*, I (Princeton, 1959), 86–87.

20. Du Voisin, *La France chrétienne*, 211–12.

21. Ibid., 100.

22. Ibid., 100–101, 135. Bossuet, *Politique tirée des propres paroles*, 228.

23. Du Voisin, *La France chrétienne*, 98.

24. See Chapter 1.

25. Beik, in *The French Revolution Seen from the Right*, 20 n. 46, thought it was completed before the summer of 1789.

26. abbé Augustin de Barruel, *Le patriote véridique, ou discours sur les vraies causes de la révolution actuelle* (Paris, 1789), 32; Bossuet, *Politique tirée des propres paroles*, 217–18.

27. Barruel, *La patriote véridique*, 94–97.

28. Ibid., 110–11.
29. Ibid., 103, 112.
30. Ibid., 115.
31. Ibid., 119, 121.
32. abbé Augustin de Barruel, *Question nationale sur l'autorité et sur les droits du peuple dans le gouvernement, ou expositon et démonstration des vraies principes sur la souveraineté* (Paris, 1791), 3.
33. Barruel here is using the analysis of Rousseau to try to combat the principles of the French Revolution. Jean-Jacques Rousseau, *Du Contrat social*, edited with an Introduction by Ronald Grimsley (Oxford, 1972), Book I, chapters 6–7, 113–18.
34. Barruel, *Question nationale sur l'autorité*, 49–50.
35. *Question nationale sur l'autorité*, 16. Marc Goldstein explained Barruel's policy here as follows: "The multitude is necessarily anarchic not only in the analytical sense whereby its role is the absence of government, but because it is preeminently atomistic. There are no common horizontal interests in Barruel's portrait of man without government; there is no foundation upon which the general welfare can be established. There are only conflicting individuals whose capacity for multiplying obstacles to the common well-being is directly proportional to their number. To the extent that the well-being of the people is considered a desirable end, to that same extent, the people must be governed," Marc A. Goldstein, *The People in French Counter-Revolutionary Thought* (New York, 1988), 32.
36. Ibid., 17.
37. Ibid., 27, 51; Bossuet, *Politique tirée des propres paroles*, 272.
38. Ibid., 57–59. As was the case with Du Voisin, the source of these ideas is Bossuet: 44, 46, 64–65, 271–72. As proof of his assertion he offered the example of the Fête de la Fédération on the Champs de Mars on July 14, 1790, though he would deny its validity. Here the French showed that they did not believe their new constitution and their supposed sovereignty was enough to establish valid authority. They felt they had to make God a witness to their adhesion to the constitution and swear an oath to uphold it. Ibid., 64–65.
39. Ibid., 97; Bossuet, *Politique tirée des propres paroles*, 65–66, 69, 92–93.
40. Barruel, *Question nationale sur l'autorité*, 97–98. Barruel here again follows Bossuet, *Politique tirée des propres paroles*, 70–71, 74–75, 77–78, 90.
41. Barruel, *Question nationale sur l'autorité*, 98. For Bossuet on fundamental laws see *Politique tirée des propres paroles*, 28.
42. Barruel, *Question nationale sur l'autorité*, 101, 104; Bossuet, *Politique tirée des propres paroles*, 92–93, 96–97.
43. Barruel, *Question nationale sur l'autorité*, 107.
44. Ibid., 108–9.
45. Rousseau, *Du Contrat social*, Book III, chapter 15, 188–92.
46. Barruel, *Question nationale sur l'autorité*, 110–12.
47. Ibid., 116; Bossuet, *Politique tirée des propres paroles*, 119–121.
48. Barruel, *Question nationale sur l'autorité*, 117.
49. *Lettre adressée au Roi . . . le 9 Fevrier 1789, Seconde lettre adressée au Roi . . . Le 5 Avril 1789, De l'état de la France, present et à venir (Octobre 1790), Tableau de l'Europe, en novembre 1795, Tableau de l'Europe, Jusqu'au commencement de 1796*. See Beik, *The French Revolution Seen from the Right*, 16–17, 43–45, 93–94.
50. *Dictionnaire de biographie française*, 7 (1956), 922–23.

51. Charles Alexandre de Calonne, *De l'état de la France tel qu'il peut et qu'il doit être; Pour faire suite à l'État de la France présent et à venir* (London, Paris, November 1790), 15.

52. Ibid., 16, 18.

53. Ibid., 21.

54. Ibid., 60.

55. Ibid., 73.

56. Ibid., 74.

57. Rivarol emigrated on June 10, 1792, and spent the remainder of his life in exile. William J. Murray, *The Right-Wing Press in the French Revolution: 1789–92*, 56–57, 177, 206; *Dictionnaire biographique des auteurs*, II (Paris, 1958), 448–49.

58. Francis Bertin, "La monarchie selon les émigrés," *Découverte*, 4 (1974), 47.

59. Quoted from the *Mercure de France*, in Claude Bellanger et al., *Histoire générale de la presse française*, I (Paris, 1969), 473.

60. These concessions put him in the camp of the constitutional monarchists. Claude Bellanger et al., *Histoire générale de la presse française*, I, 474; Murray, *The Right-Wing Press in the French Revolution: 1789–92*, 13, 16.

61. Ibid., 243.

62. Ibid., 246.

63. Bellanger et al., *Histoire générale de la presse française*, I, 474, which speculates that Rivarol inspired Burke to write his *Reflections on the Revolution in France*. William J. Murray in his thorough study of the right-wing press said that the *Journal politique national* did not have as much influence on Rivarol's contemporaries as its quotation by subsequent historians leads one to believe. It was successful, and it made Rivarol wealthy. However, it came out irregularly and at a time when many other journalists were clamoring for attention. And it was written only for an elite; Rivarol was not one to pander to the crowd. Moreover, it offered violent opinion, rather than a careful analysis of the National Assembly. It has been highly quoted because Rivarol was such an excellent stylist. His ideas anticipated Burke, and his style set the example for Taine. Murray, *The Right-Wing Press*, 56–57.

64. Bellanger et al., *Histoire générale de la presse française*, I, 475–76; J. Gilchrist and W. J. Murray, eds., *The Press in the French Revolution: A Selection of Documents Taken from the Press of the Revolution for the Years 1789–1794* (New York, 1971), 22; William J. Murray, *The Right-Wing Press*, 52–55.

65. *Actes des Apôtres*, VI, 174, quoted from Bellanger et al., *Histoire générale de la presse française*, I, 477.

66. Bellanger et al., *Histoire générale de la presse française*, I, 479, 482; Murray, *The Right-Wing Press*, 31–34.

67. Bellanger et al., *Histoire générale de la presse française*, I, 483.

68. William J. Murray, "The Right-Wing Press in the French Revolution," Ph.D. dissertation (Australian National University, 1971), 15.

69. *Gazette de Paris*, June 4, 1790.

70. Ibid.

71. Gilchrist and Murray, eds., *The Press in the French Revolution*, 23; Bellanger et al., *Histoire générale de la presse française*, 482.

72. *Gazette de Paris*, January 1, 1791.

73. Bellanger et al., *Histoire générale de la presse française*, I, 482–83; Murray, *The Right-Wing Press*, 31–34, 182–83, 285–88.

74. Murray, "The Right-Wing Press in the French Revolution," 17; William J. Murray, *The Right-Wing Press*, 34.

75. Murray, *The Right-Wing Press*, 35–40; Bellanger et al., *Histoire générale de la presse française*, I, 483–85.

76. *L'Ami du Roi* (Royou), September 28, 1790.

77. His remarks were sparked by debates in the National Assembly on March 26 and March 28, 1791, on the powers of the King. The first session was on the regency for a minor king; the second on where the King might reside. See *Réimpression de l'Ancien Moniteur*, VI (Paris, 1861), 724–26, 746–54.

78. Bossuet, *Politique tirée des propres paroles*, 51–52, 64–65.

79. Royou may have made use of Rousseau, who said that luxury in a democracy "takes away from the State all its citizens, to enslave them one to another, and all to opinion," *Du Contrat social*, Grimsley ed., Book III, chapter 4, 164. Grimsley in turn cites Montesquieu, *Esprit des lois*, VII, 1.

80. *L'Ami du Roi* (Royou), March 30, 1791; Murray, *The Right-Wing Press*, 239–40; Bossuet, *Politique tirée des propres paroles*, 52–55, 56–58.

81. *L'Ami du Roi* (Royou), March 31, 1791.

82. *Année littéraire*, nos. 41, 44, 45 (1789), *L'Ami du Roi* (November 14, 1790), as cited in Murray, *The Right-Wing Press*, 242–43.

83. *L'Ami du Roi* (Royou), March 21, 1791, in Gilchrist and Murray, eds. and trans., *The Press in the French Revolution*, 164–65.

84. Murray, *The Right-Wing Press*, 244.

85. Murray, "The Right-Wing Press in the French Revolution," 446–47; Murray, *The Right-Wing Press*, 246.

86. Suleau, however, did not draw the implication that they had not been properly fed at the end of the Old Regime.

87. Murray, "The Right-Wing Press in the French Revolution," 450–52, 481.

88. Quoted from Gilchrist and Murray, eds., *The Press in the French Revolution*, 207–8.

89. Bossuet had the same idea, though he did not express it as strongly: "God inspires obedience in peoples and dissipates a spirit of insurrection," Bossuet, *Politique tirée des propres paroles*, 272.

90. Cited from Gerard Walter, ed., *La Révolution française vue par ses journaux* (Paris, 1948), 117, 118, 122–23. He held to the same postion in the issue of December 22, 1790: "Counter-revolution by force thus seems a chimera. Let us leave it to time which destroys all, except for that which should remain. The laws that passions have dictated will destroy themselves; the others will work for our welfare, with the good prince that the heavens have given us." Ibid., 136. It wasn't until about the time of the Declaration of Pillnitz that he took the counter-revolution seriously. *L'Ami du Roi* (Royou), September 3 and 6, 1791.

91. Murray, *The Right-Wing Press*, 252–53.

92. Guillaume Marie Anne Brune, the future marshal of France, founded it on September 16, 1789, as the *Journal général de la Cour et de la Ville*. In October he took on Jacques Louis Gautier de Syonnet as a collaborator. They soon quarreled and beginning December 16 two papers appeared under the same name. Brune's paper stopped publication on January 2, 1790, and Gautier's paper carried on as the *Journal de la Cour et de la Ville* until August 10, 1792. Bellanger et al., *Histoire générale de la presse française*, 471–73; Gilchrist and Murray, eds., *The Press in the French Revolution*, 22–23; Murray, *The Right-Wing Press*, 49–52.

93. *Journal de la Cour et de la Ville*, April 3, 1791.

94. *Journal de la Cour et de la Ville*, June 24, 1791, as cited from Walter, ed., *La Révolution française vue par ses journaux*, 179.

95. *L'Ami du Roi* (Royou), June 28–29, 1791, as cited from Walter, ed., *La Révolution française vue par ses journaux*, 180–97. An anonymous pamphlet issued in 1791, *Adresse aux Français*, made some of the same points and also denied that Louis XVI had been carried away from Paris against his will.

96. Cited from *Ami du Roi* (Royou), July 2, 1791.

97. Emmanuel Louis, comte d'Antraigues, *Point d'accommodement*.

CHAPTER III

French Royalist Thought, 1791–1792

French royalists writing during the period of the Legislative Assembly (1791–1792) were still preoccupied with the causes of the French Revolution. Most of their explanations were simplistic: the Revolution stemmed from a conspiracy, though they did not always agree on who the conspirators were. Sometimes it was the Freemasons or the philosophes; sometimes those two groups plus the Jansenists and the Protestants.[1] A variation on this theme was that the Old Regime might have saved itself if it had co-opted the men of letters, instead of letting them vent their frustration by allying with hostile outside forces. But the most original idea was that the Revolution developed from the opposition to the monarchy offered by the aristocrats.

Besides accounting for the Revolution, the Right also tried to rally support for the King. Here they were not successful, in part because political trends ran so strongly against the King during this period, in part because Louis XVI lacked political sense and skill, but also because royalist writers themselves demonstrated a lack of political experience and inventiveness. So their calls for Frenchmen to rally around the King went largely unheeded. While France was in the midst of its first experiment with limited constitutional monarchy, they argued that it could never be governed by a legislature and that it should return to the principles of 1789, if not those of 1614. Some even went so far as to resurrect the divine right of kings! Their strongest argument was that the King was the best defender of order and prosperity. In the end they sought to use war, as did the King himself, as a last desperate means to restore the King's position and to crush his foes.

The abbé Jacques François Lefranc (1739–1792) explained the French Revolution by singling out the Freemasons. In *Le voile levé pour les curieux* (1791), Lefranc claimed that the fabric of French society and government had been weakened by the Masonic movement. As proof he argued that the National Assembly had pushed Masonic projects with all its power: "the National Assembly, while saying that it wanted a monarchical government, that the king had never been more a king than he would be by its decrees, nevertheless finished by adopting a republican government and a pure democracy. And it borrowed the organization from Freemasonry."[2]

Lefranc went on to assert that Freemasonry aimed at overthrowing both the throne and the altar, in fact any authority that was not subject to it. Wanting to eliminate royalty, it destroyed every institution that supported it. And if those following the dictates of Freemasonry in the National Assembly did preserve the title of king, it only meant as much as the title of grand master in the Masons. Like the grand master, the king now held his title from his brothers, who could take it away from him or could keep him in office according to their pleasure. The point was that henceforth the king was dependent on the wishes of those who granted his authority.[3]

By 1792 Lefranc's conspiracy theory had become more elaborate. Now he described an alliance of Freemasons, philosophes, Protestants, Jansenists, atheists, and the impious, who attacked Catholicism at the end of the Old Regime and then turned their guns on the monarchy during the French Revolution.[4] What was involved here, he believed, was a struggle for the very soul of man. "Philosophy, arrogant reason, error, and falsehood want to occupy the space in all hearts. To achieve that objective they want the earth soaked with the blood of kings and priests."[5]

And he closed with a warning that France offered a horrible example of what would happen to any nation that protected sectarians and modern philosophies. It would find authority overthrown, the throne dashed to bits, crime unpunished, property invaded, innocence oppressed, and vice honored. Intrigue, pride, and self-interest, sustained by crime and injustice, would triumph.[6]

The comte de Barruel-Beauvert (1756–1817), a former soldier who became a counter-revolutionary publicist at the time of the Revolution, was another recruit to the conspiracy camp. He also pointed his finger at the philosophy of the eighteenth century, which he thought had destroyed conscience and stirred up all the passions. After undermining religion, Barruel-Beauvert believed that philosophy was determined to destroy monarchy throughout Europe. In fact he saw them engaged in a mortal combat: either the new philosophy would eliminate the monarchy or the monarchs would destroy philosophy. Kings would remain strong if they armed themselves promptly to maintain the old laws, to repress all illegal innovations, and to punish all wrongdoers. In so doing they would preserve their people from "the moral frenzy that dissolves Empires. . . ." Otherwise the kings would soon face "a general corruption of principles and opinions," which would turn their people into a "frightening assemblage of evil and criminal men," and would exalt baseness and infamy.[7]

But it was really the periodical press that had more original and interesting views on the causes of the French Revolution during this period. This was particularly the case of a new newspaper, the *Journal-Pie*, founded by Claude François Rivarol (1762–1848) on January 16, 1792.[8] On January 28, an article appeared in it claiming that the Revolution would never have taken place if the government had co-opted the men of letters by finding places for them in the government. Prominent writers, like La Harpe and Suard, should have been made farmers-general. Lesser lights, who were dying of hunger and making other people die of pity, should have been found places in the departments, where they would have served the useful function of destroying seditious philosophy, which fed on misery and which never resisted the lure of favor and fortune.[9]

Even more important was the *Journal-Pie's* explanation of the aristocratic resurgence as having caused the French Revolution.[10] In its January 22 issue, the newspaper reported that when the King convened the Notables and asked for an increase in taxation, the parlements, the clergy, and the upper nobility became the true enemies of the monarchy. A number of colonels even went so far as to swear that they would not order their troops to move against the parlements, while the parlements, as in the days of the Fronde, claimed that they were acting in the public interest, though actually looking out for their own particular advantage. In fact it was the three privileged bodies that caused the disaster, including the calling of the Estates-General.[11]

This account was followed by a scathing February 1 attack on the aristocracy. Louis XVI, the author asserted, must have had an exceedingly high opinion of men if he believed that the privileged bodies wanted to put him back on the throne for his own sake. The aristocrats, who lacked all self-control when they spoke of the King, said that he was more responsible for the disasters than the Constituant Assembly—a patent untruth. What the aristocrats should have said was that they made the Revolution necessary by their refusal to sanction taxes. True royalists, the author went on, were convinced that the aristocrats were only interested in regaining their privileges, including the feudal system if possible; that the clergy thought only of its wealth; and that what the parlements wanted was the right once more to deliver their high-handed remonstrances.[12]

Besides explaining why the Revolution had come about, royalists spent a great deal of time trying to promote the monarchy. The royalist newspaper, *Journal de M. Suleau*, for example, presented a very bleak picture of France early in 1792. According to that paper France was completely disorganized, offering a picture of unrelieved chaos. In this situation the Constitution of 1791 offered absolutely no protection. To remedy the situation the Legislative Assembly first had to invest the King with the widest possible powers so that he could negotiate with foreign powers, who had legitimate grievances against France. After those discussions the legislature had to declare itself a constituent assembly and revise the constitution. The *Journal* did not indicate how to do this, but it was confident that a majority of the people would support constitutional change.

Suleau also presented a very negative assessment of the economic situation. The navy had been abandoned, the army was in disarray, the economy was bringing prosperity only to foreign countries, and commerce was on its last legs.

"Nevertheless, the resources of all kinds are so fecund, our soil so productive, our industry so profitable, we are besides so powerfully favored by our topographical position that, if we employ as much activity in closing up our wounds as with frenzy we employed in tearing ourselves to pieces, the pustules of anarchy soon will be no more than honorable stygmata of the conquest of liberty."[13]

Suleau also foresaw a solution to French social tensions. It wasn't as difficult as one thought to lessen hatred, extinguish resentment, and to rally everyone toward a common center. One could resolve the tensions between those in France and the émigrés by some equitable arrangement that would allow the émigrés to forget the evils of the past and return to France. Without striking a blow or shedding a drop of blood, somehow this would end the dissensions and restore harmony.[14]

The *Journal-Pie* defined as true royalists those who wanted to reform the old abuses and the current excesses, and who loved the King because he was king and because he was virtuous. It warned against confusing those with what it described as constitutional royalists, who loved the constitution more than the King. True royalists, according to this account, had as much disdain for the aristocrats, who wanted to revise feudalism, as they did for the Jacobins, who wanted a republic, because both positions were impossible. The same issue rejected impartiality in such a time of crisis, calling those who tried to be impartial "imbeciles." Anyone who tried to serve as a moderator had not realized that in a time of great agitation one must "speak with passion and not with reason."[15]

Later in the year, after the war had begun, Antoine Rivarol (1753–1801), brother of Charles François Rivarol, addressed a letter to the French nobles who were returning to France under the command of the Duke of Brunswick, warning them to follow the orders of the King and not to try to stake out an independent political position. He advised them that in France they were not sovereign, as were the nobles in Germany, nor feudal as those in Poland, nor legislators as in England, nor a sacred caste as in India. They were instead men of honor who should live and die under the command of the King. Rivarol warned that if they did not follow the lead of the King, they would set off a new revolution.[16]

The comte d'Antraigues, a leading figure in the counter-revolution, also sought to defend the monarchy as he understood it. Antraigues argued that France already had a legal constitution, and only the Estates-General and the King could establish another. Anything else was illegal, the result of force, the work of tyrants. The only legal constitution was that of 1614, to which France had to return.[17]

The comte Armand d'Allonville (1762–ca. 1832) claimed that the French constitution had existed for 400 years and that during that time, despite numerous revolutions, there had been no changes in its original structure. Furthermore, he maintained that the people, to the extent that they had not been corrupted, supported this system. This structure, in fact, was the only way to achieve happiness and liberty. The prescription Allonville offered in May of 1792 was to return to the royal program of June 23, 1789. Although it was not perfect, its adoption would immediately produce a magical change in France's fortunes.[18]

Christophe Montjoie (1746–1816), editor of a version of the royalist newspaper *L'Ami du Roi*, 1790–1792, added his voice to those of Antraigues and Allonville in calling for a restoration of the old order. An almanac put out by his paper in 1792 made the following assertions: "The character of the French nation cannot support any other government but pure monarchy, slightly tempered by the resistance of the orders in their remonstrances and representations. One should not hide the fact that the French are too inconstant, too ignorant, and even too wicked to give themselves a government of several masters."[19] The almanac went on to say that legislators and administrators would never provide the stability, the enterprise, or the strength necessary to govern. The King and the orders were the only government appropriate to France.

The final person included in this section who advocated a return to the old constitution was General Charles Tinseau d'Amondans (1749–1822), author of *Nouveau plan de constitution* of 1792. Tinseau d'Amondans, like the comte d'Allonville, argued for a return to the ideas contained in Louis XVI's declaration of June 23, 1789. According to Tinseau it consisted of the old government corrected of abuses and restored to its first principles.[20]

Tinseau was a constitutional monarchist, interested in using the Estates-General to circumscribe the power of the king, and to promote the rights and privileges of the first two orders. But he recognized the power of the king to convene and dissolve the Estates-General and to rule certain subjects out of order, and he insisted that the nation wanted it to exist and would never consider as constitutional any measure put through without its approval.[21]

Tinseau also argued that it was in the interest of the kings to assemble the Estates-General frequently. He claimed that if it met infrequently and was only convened in times of emergency, the French, who were by nature unstable and restless, would have exaggerated hopes for it. They would consider it as a panacea for all their problems. But if it met often and in ordinary times, then the indifference of the French for everything familiar would help them put it in proper perspective. They would realize that it was made up of representatives of landowners, who gathered to grant the taxes necessary for the needs of the state, and to set forth and obtain redress for the grievances of the people. In short, the French would come to see it as a normal institution of government.[22]

Louis Fontenai's *Journal général* defended the monarchy on the grounds that republicanism was incompatible with the customs, the character, and the extent of the French Empire. And, long before the Declaration of Pillnitz, this paper provided an explicit warning that Paris would suffer greatly if it harmed the King or any member of the royal family.[23]

A few weeks later Fontenai returned to this subject and again called upon the Parisians to rally around the King and the royal family. This was the surest way to guarantee their property and their persons. He repeated that they would have nothing left if they disturbed the tranquility of the King. One had to realize, he said, that revolutionaries were employing horrible means to lead people to excess. They were feeding them lies to distract their attention from the defense of their property.[24]

The most amazing rationale for the monarchy came in appeals, as late as 1792, for the divine right of kings. They appeared in January in De Rozoi's *Gazette de Paris* and then in July in the *Journal général*. The latter reached back and quoted a sermon of the abbé Torné of 1764, which said that kings should be obeyed and that resisting kings was the same as resisting God. Furthermore, the abbé had asserted that subjects had to remain faithful to their ruler no matter how much oppression they suffered, and that no one had the right to question the king about his rule.[25]

One of the most trenchant of the royalist journalists was Louis François Suleau (1758–1792), who first made a name for himself as a contributor to the scandalous *Actes des Apôtres* in 1790 and then published his own *Journal de M. Suleau* (March 1791 to April 1792).[26]

Suleau above all was an activist. He did not always know what course to pursue and his advice was not consistent, but he did believe in pursuing with great vigor whatever seemed appropriate at the moment. And he was particularly directive in his advice to Louis XVI, whom he tried to get off what Suleau regarded as dead center. In the aftermath of the 1789 October Days, he promised the King 1,200,000 defenders, ready to give their blood. But he called on the King to stop putting up with the affronts and the insults of those who were trying to destroy his authority. "Don't you ever dare," he asked impatiently, "to decide and act for yourself? Descend majestically into the middle of your people, not to mingle your tears with the blood of the victims of their vengeance, but to signify to them that you have firmly decided to live and to die as a king!"[27]

Once he had his own newspaper, his tone showed no sign of mellowing. This was his message in the spring of 1791:

> Moved by a righteous indignation, eager to swell the host of true defenders of the fatherland, I waited for the signal for the battle to begin; I asked for the successor of Henry the Great; I looked for the panache that would show us road to honor and victory . . . You appeared, and I saw a slave who dolefully bore the irons upon his unjust hands that a barbarous and sacrilegious troop had manacled. . . . Your people has seated itself on your throne; your people has invaded every authority; your people has declared itself your sovereign. . . . Louis, recover as a man that liberty that you lost as a king. . . . remember that it is better to be THE FIRST OF MEN THAN THE LAST OF KINGS.[28]

In the fall of 1791, when he was in exile at Coblentz, Suleau tried to win Louis XVI over to the side of the princes, telling him that he would get nowhere cooperating with the revolutionaries. Now was the time for the King to throw himself into the arms of his brothers, who had the firm intention and all the necessary means to save Louis XVI from himself. And, according to Suleau, there were no grounds for suspecting the motives of the princes. All they wanted was to restore the King to power and then set an example by their submission and their obedience.[29]

Then late in 1791 or early in 1792, while still in exile, he made a prediction that the French Revolution would lead to despotism, and in fact he looked forward to it because only despotism would save France from anarchy. Despotism would cauterize its wounds and reunite a great empire that had fallen into dissolution. And what France needed was not the suppleness of a Mazarin, but "the lordly inflexibility of a Richelieu."[30]

In February of 1792, disgusted with the émigrés, Suleau returned to Paris. In the spring of 1792, in one of his last issues, after describing Louis XVI as too indulgent and too patient, and after announcing that there was no hope for deliverance from Coblentz, he urged Louis XVI to faithfully execute the Constitution of 1791, which would ultimately prove itself unworkable and devour its authors.[31] After advocating almost every conceivable course, Suleau ended up calling for war and for the victory of the allied powers against France.[32]

The royalist press as a whole hoped that the King could take advantage of the war clouds to strengthen his own position. Following the defensive alliance between Austria and Prussia, on February 7, 1792, the *Journal de la Cour et de la Ville*, edited by Guillaume Brune and Jacques Louis Gautier de Syonnet, reported that France was menaced "by all the powers of Europe." In this situation one had to rally around the King, "make a rampart of our bodies," restore his authority, uphold it, and use it to crush the rebels in France.[33]

Then in March, the abbé Royou published *L'Ami du Roi* in which he asserted the death of Emperor Leopold II and the succession of Frances II would hasten the coming of war—which he eagerly looked forward to. It described Francis as young, strongly opposed to the Revolution, anxious to establish a name for himself, and passionately interested in the military. It added that the exiled Bourbon princes thought their cause had never been in a more favorable position.[34]

As war approached, however, the constitutional monarchist *Feuille du jour* took a different tack. On April 20, the day France declared war, it urged all Frenchmen, revolutionaries and counter-revolutionaries, to work together to save the country, which was in danger. In an elaborate metaphor it compared the situation of France to that of a group of people on a sinking ship in stormy seas. On this ship everyone wanted to command, and no one to obey. The compass was broken; the rudder wouldn't work. The passengers were in the greatest danger. It then asked whether the French would make their situation worse, rather than helping to save each other. It was no longer important whether some had been aristocrats, democrats, Jacobins, Feuillants, royalists, republicans, or constitutionals. What one had to do was to save the ship of state. Each person, working to save the life of his neighbor, at the same time was helping to save his own. Now was the time for survival; afterwards they could discuss and would probably find that they agreed.[35]

But most of the royalist papers, including *L'Ami du Roi*, persisted in thinking only about what advantage the King could draw from the war. Commenting on Dumouriez' April 20 speech outlining the reasons for war, *L'Ami du Roi* described this as a war of kings against factions and incendiaries, and said that either all the kings would perish or they would exterminate the brigands who were opposed to all authority and all government. It was not the misfortunes of the émigrés that stirred them into action, but a sense of their own danger. Hence it was no longer a French problem, but a European one, and help for the King must come from outside.[36]

In June the *Gazette de Paris* actually published an appeal from the émigrés at Coblentz for funds to help support the counter-revolution. They explained that the French princes had armed them, but that more money was needed. "The justice of our cause, the zeal that inspires our courage, and the support of all Europe, guarantee our success. . . . The public cause demands that we gather and assemble together all that can serve to redeem it from the rebels' hands. We have no other aim; no mixture of vindictive sentiment sullies the purity of our intentions; *zeal for Religion, fidelity to the King, love of Country*, these are our only motives."[37]

But that tone did not last very long. As the allies advanced in the latter part of July, the *Gazette de Paris* predicted that the victory of the counter-revolutionaries would lead not only to the return of the ancient constitution and the restoration of the property and privileges of the clergy and the nobility, but also to a thorough punishment of the political factions. The first town to resist the counter-revolutionaries would be razed and any revolutionaries in the army "would be hanged on the spot."[38] Following the publication of the Brunswick Manifesto on August 3, 1792, the *Journal de la Cour et de la Ville* warned the Parisians that they had to atone for the June 20 demonstration against the King. And they had to make up their minds quickly about what course they were going to take, because the Duke of Brunswick was coming. The implication left was that now the enemies of the King would be punished severely![39]

The counter-revolutionary newspapers thus openly hoped for the victory of the émigrés and the allies. They even went so far as to tell the enemy about the organization, route, and the camps of the French army. At the same time extremism was rising in the revolutionary camp. When the revolutionaries won on August 10, the royalists paid the price: their papers were suppressed and their journalists convicted of treason.[40]

Thus during this period French royalists paid some attention to why the Revolution took place. They continued to develop the conspiracy theory of history, which conveniently blamed all the problems on outside agitators. But they also demonstrated an understanding of the importance of recruiting men of letters in the battle for public support. And the *Journal-Pie* pointed the finger at the aristocrats, and said that by their arrogant demands they were the ones responsible for starting the Revolution.

Monarchists spent most of their time trying to defend the old order and to hasten its restoration. But they were divided among themselves, and they tended to ignore contemporary political realities and to engage in a good deal of wishful thinking. They argued that monarchy was the *only* form of government appropriate to the French people and to French traditions. They said that France had had a working constitution for hundreds of years—there was no need to go out and try to get another one. They went so far as to try to invoke the divine right of kings. Royalists portrayed the King as a barrier to the return of feudalism, though this must have seemed a very dim possibility in 1792. But their most telling arguments followed a utilitarian rationale: the King was best because he could best promote internal order and prosperity, ease social tensions, and make peace with France's neighbors. In all this they made a contribution to the formation of modern conservatism. But when all else seemed to fail they foolishly turned to threats, which deepened political antagonisms and prepared the way for their fall, along with that of the monarchy.

It was really François Suleau in his calls for action that set the royalist tone for the latter part of this period. After trying in vain to get Louis XVI moving, he rolled up his sleeves, called for war, and looked forward to the victory of the allies. Others followed the same course. The threat of war made them call for a restoration of the King's authority. They appealed for funds for the émigrés. They looked to foreign kings for salvation. In an atmosphere of amazing freedom of the press, they not only contributed to a heightening of political tensions, but also stepped across the line to treason.[41] But, by threatening their countrymen with retribution, they failed to realize that they were playing with political dynamite. When the explosion came, they went down before it.

NOTES

An earlier version of this chapter was delivered at the Consortium on Revolutionary Europe, 1988, and published in the *Proceedings of the Consortium on Revolutionary Europe*, 18 (1988), 95–110.

1. The classic accounts here were provided by the abbé Augustin de Barruel: *La patriote véridique, ou discours sur les vraies causes de la révolution actuelle* (1789); *Question nationale sur l'autorité et sur les droits du peuple dans le gouvernement . . .* (1791); *Histoire du clergé pendant la révolution françoise* (1793); *Mémoires pour servir à l'histoire du jacobinisme*, 4 vols. (1797–1798).

2. abbé Jacques François Lefranc, *Le voile levé pour les curieux*, (n.p., 1791), 57–58.

3. *Le voile levé pour les curieux*, 54–55.

4. The alliance described here was later used by the abbé Barruel in his *Mémoires pour servir à l'histoire du jacobinisme* (1797–1798); abbé Jacques François Lefranc, *Conjuration contre la religion catholique et les souverains, dont le projet, conçu en France, doit s'exécuter dans l'univers entier, ouvrage utile à tous les Français* (Paris, 1792), 20.

5. *Conjuration contre la religion catholique et les souverains*, 138.

6. Ibid., 353.

7. *Nouvelle Biographie Générale*, 4 (1853), vol. 601; Antoine Joseph, comte de Barruel-Beauvert, *Première Collection du Journal royaliste, depuis le 16 mars 1792 jusques au 14 juin inclusivement (et depuis le 16 juin 1792 jusques au 9 aout 1792)*, II (Paris, July 20, 1792), 7.

8. Claude François Rivarol was the brother of the more well-known journalist and writer, Antoine Rivarol. Claude François turned the editorship of his new paper over to the comte de Barruel-Beauvert in March of 1792. William J. Murray, *The Right-Wing Press in the French Revolution 1789–92* (Woodbridge, Eng., 1986), 167–68.

9. *Journal-Pie*, January 28, 1792. This piece may have been written by Antoine Rivarol because it sounds similar to an account he published in the *Journal Politique-National* on August 9, 1789:

> It is indisputable that the Books of the Philosophes did not do anything by themselves since the People did not read them and did not know them. But it is no less true that they were very harmful by all the Books that they inspired and that the People very well understood. A brochure such as the *Orateur aux États Généraux*, which is only a disgusting paraphrase of several lines of the *Social Contract*, was spread incredibly among the lower class who had never read the *Social Contract*. In other times a book which did not pass through the antechamber was not dangerous; today in effect there are only those who do not leave the antechambers that are truly to be feared. In this one must admire the Philosophes who write with elevation to correct Governments and not to overthrow them, to help the people and not to raise them up. But the Governments scorned the voice of the great Writers and gave time to little spirits to begin works of Genius and to put them at the disposal of the Populace.

10. An idea I have first found stated in Gabriel Sénac de Meilhan's *Des Principes et des causes de la Révolution en France* (London, 1790), 78–79.

11. *Journal-Pie*, January 22, 1792.

12. *Journal-Pie*, February 1, 1792.

13. *Journal de M. Suleau*, no. XI, in Gérard Walter, ed., *La Révolution française vue par ses journaux* (Paris, [1948]), 218–20. On this newspaper see William J. Murray, *The Right-Wing Press in the French Revolution, 1789–92*, 59–60.

14. Ibid.

15. *Journal-Pie*, January 16, 1792.

16. Antoine Rivarol, "Lettre à la noblesse francaise, au moment de sa rentre en France, sous les ordres de m. le duc de Brunswick . . ." (1792), in *Écrits et pamphlets de Rivarol . . . recue-illis pour la première fois et annotés par A. P. Mailassis* (Paris, 1877), 135–36.

17. comte d'Antraigues, *Exposé de notre antique et seule légale constitution française* (Paris, March 15, 1792), 8, 57.

18. comte Armand d'Allonville, *Lettre d'un royaliste à M. Malouet, du mardi 22 mai 1792* (Paris, 1792), 4–5, 18; *Dictionnaire de biographie française*, II (1936), col. 234.

19. Christophe Félix Louis Ventre de la Touloubre Montjoie, *L'Ami du roi, almanach des honnêtes gens, avec des prophètes pour chaque moi de l'année* (Paris [1792]), 31–32.

20. Charles Marie Thérèse Léon Tinseau d'Amondans, *Nouveau plan de constitution, presenté par les émigrès, à la nation françoise, ou Essai sur les deux déclarations du Roi, Faites les 23 Juin 1789; sur les modifications à y faire pour qu'elles puissent servir de*

bases du Gouv. François; et sur la nécessité de les proposer le plus promptement possible a l'acceptation des États-Généraux (Worms, 1792), 9; Elphège Boursin and Augustin Challamel, eds., *Dictionnaire de la Révolution française, Institutions, hommes et faits* (Paris, 1893), 825.

21. Tinseau d'Amondans, *Nouveau plan de constitution*, 10.

22. Ibid., 13–14.

23. *Journal générale*, May 6, 1792. On the *Journal générale*, see Murray, *The Right-Wing Press in the French Revolution: 1789–92*, 45–47, 164–65, 236.

24. *Journal général*, May 30, 1792.

25. *Gazette de Paris*, January 6, 1792, as cited in Lynn Hunt, *Politics, Culture, and Class in the French Revolution* (Berkeley, 1984), 88; *Journal général*, July 12, 1792. On the *Gazette de Paris* see Murray, *The Right-Wing Press*, 78–81, 183, 236–37.

26. For details on his revolutionary career, see J. Gilchrist and W. J. Murray, eds., *The Press in the French Revolution: A Selection of Documents taken from the Press of the Revolution for the Years 1789–1794* (New York, 1971), 25; Claude Bellanger, Jacques Godechot, Pierre Guiral, and Fernand Terrou, eds., *Histoire générale de la presse française*, I (Paris, 1969), 478–79; René de Livois, *Histoire de la presse française*, I (Paris, 1965), 96–99; and especially Murray, *The Right-Wing Press*, 58–60.

27. François Louis Suleau, *Un petit mot à Louis XVI sur les crimes de ses vertus et l'insuffisance pour le bonheur de son people de la pureté de ses voeux et de la rectitude de ses intentions* (n.p., 1789), in Marcel Frager, *Le fulgurant monsieur Suleau, 1758–1792* (Paris [1945]), 41.

28. *Journal de M. Suleau*, no. 2, as quoted in Gilchrist and Murray, eds., *The Press in the French Revolution*, 142–43.

29. Bernard de Vaulx, ed., *Journal de François Suleau, le chevalier de la difficulté et écrits divers* (Paris, 1946), 45–47.

30. Ibid., 53–55.

31. *Journal de M. Suleau*, no. 12, April, 1792.

32. Bellanger et al., *Histoire générale de la presse française*, I, 479; William J. Murray, "The Right-Wing Press in the French Revolution (1789–1792), Ph.D. dissertation (Australian National University, 1971), 43.

33. *Journal de la Cour et de la Ville*, February 29, 1792. On this paper see Murray, *The Right-Wing Press*, 49–52, 86.

34. *L'Ami du Roi* (Royou), March 23, 1792. On Royou's *L'Ami du Roi* see William J. Murray, *The Right-Wing Press*, 81–83.

35. *Feuille du jour*, April 20, 1792, as cited from Gérard Walter, ed., *La Révolution française vue par ses journaux* (Paris [1948]), 230–31. On the *Feuille du Jour*, Murray, *The Right-Wing Press*, 61–62.

36. *L'Ami du Roi* (Royou), April 22, 1792.

37. Gilchrist and Murray, eds., *The Press in the French Revolution*, 144–45.

38. Murray, *The Right-Wing Press*, 184.

39. *Journal de la Cour et de la Ville*, August 4, 1792.

40. Bellanger et al., *Histoire générale de la presse française*, I, 501–2. William J. Murray characterized statements in the right-wing press about the war as follows:

> The revolutionaries were left in no doubt about the fare that awaited them if the counter-revolution was successful. The appeal to violence was no invention of Marat or the Jacobins; indeed the vio-

lence of the Left, to be institutionalized in the machinery of the Terror, had the justification of national defence; the threats of the Right were motivated largely out of vengeance. Moreover the spectacle of French people rejoicing over the defeat of their countrymen is an unedifying one by any standard, whether it be in the prominent display of foreign troop movements and their expected time of arrival in Paris, or the sneers of Gautier [de Syonnet in the *Journal de la Cour et de la Ville*] that the French could only fight if the odds were 50–1 in their favour and who mocked the early defeats as being caused by cowardice . . .

The Right-Wing Press, 185.

41. Ibid.

CHAPTER IV

Royalism During the Terror

Because the French royalist press was muzzled during the Reign of Terror, from 1793–1794, in order to discover what French conservatives were thinking it is necessary to review the few things they were able to publish outside France. This chapter will focus on two of the more significant statements, those of the comte de Ferrand and the abbé Sabatier de Castres.

Antoine François Claude, comte de Ferrand (1751–1825), was a former member of the Parlement of Paris, who emigrated in September of 1789, joined the Prince de Condé, and was admitted to the comte de Provence's Council of Regency in 1793.[1] In that year he published *Le Rétablissement de la monarchie*, in which he argued that the clergy should get back their property, the nobility their seignorial and honorific rights, and the magistrates their offices. He claimed that the King could easily correct all the old abuses. And he called for the cancellation of all the revolutionary decrees and the restoration of the King's power.[2]

He then turned his attention to the causes of the French Revolution, he first cited the fact that the King's ministers had been changed too frequently, resulting in a dangerous fluctuation of principles. Even worse was the fact that the ministers had not enforced the laws. To correct abuses France needed not new laws, but implementation of the old ones.[3]

But more basically he decried the Enlightenment, which had attacked the truths of religion, the basis of all social truths. Religion, which taught humility and submission to authority and that the failure or the success of government was the result of divine punishment or blessing, "was the most firm support of sovereigns and the strongest bond of subjects." Since morality was based on religion, the blows of the philosophes against religion led to the abandonment of moral principles. They undermined true morality, put up a brilliant façade, and left behind a legacy of egotism.[4]

In explaining why the Revolution occurred, Ferrand again turned his attention to politics and cited the abuses in government finance. The debt, which was already going up, increased rapidly during the War for American Independence. Revenues, though increased, could not keep up. Costs had to be cut, though the wealth of France far surpassed its needs, as the excessive expenditures during the Revolution proved. Reform was easy, and all those in the government, from

Louis XVI on down, were dedicated to achieving it.[5] But there was a related problem: there were too many people who had loaned money to the government and too many speculators who had a vested interest in the government's being in debt.[6]

At this time the government should have realized that the deficit in public morality was even greater than that in finances, and it should have proceeded to enact reforms on its own authority. Since the unity of the state was already disturbed, the government needed to move swiftly and decisively. It should *not* have assembled the notables, much less the Estates-General.[7] Instead, there was a failure of nerve, and chaos ensued. The problem was compounded by revealing the details of the government's financial problems.

Ferrand blamed the Parlement for promoting the agitation for the Estates-General. The Parlement, believing that it should go along with the desires of the people and tired of registering one decree after another for laws and taxes, whose purpose was unknown, cleared the way for those who had sworn to overthrow it. All the judges followed its example, and the call for the Estates-General became universal.[8]

The faults of the ministry aggravated the situation. And the more arbitrary the government became, the more resistance to it increased. The orders and the corps became carried away by their hatred of the ministers. Almost everyone regarded authority as a hostile force, "forgetting that it was the only force that could protect them."[9]

In this crisis Loménie de Brienne decided to stir up and arm the Third Estate against the other two orders. To facilitate this program, as if it were not free enough already, he removed the last restrictions on the press. Beyond that, he stirred up a frenzy of opinion by inviting everyone to enlighten or mislead the government on how to organize the Estates-General, as if it were a historical question that could be resolved in the libraries by people who were determined to overthrow the state. The result was to unleash a deluge of animosity, intrigue, fanaticism, and delirium.[10]

And the Protestants were also in the plot. They had tried and failed to destroy the monarchy and the Catholic religion in the sixteenth century, and were resolved to try again, even though Louis XVI had guaranteed "their peace, their fortunes, their families, and their civil position." Even though most Protestants were more faithful followers of religion than were the Catholics, their hatred of the Catholic Church reconciled them to the atheists, who always supported them in their writings, not because they agreed with them but because they were opposed to truth. Atheists called for help for Protestants in the name of toleration. And the philosophes also protected them as a means of attacking religion.[11]

Then several political factions stepped in to facilitate the task, those of the duc d'Orléans,[12] of Necker, and finally of the republicans. Necker hated the clergy, who had discovered the secret of his Protestatism, the nobility, who offended his pride as a commoner, and the magistrates, who had unmasked his projects. He thought that in making these orders unpopular to the people he would attract popular support to himself. He was in a very strong position because of his apparent control of a financial situation that had gotten out of hand. The only thing that he feared was the strength of the army, so he sent it the most ambiguous orders; hence it remained passive in the wake of the popular insurrections. So the people were given free reign, and the authority of the government was allowed to collapse.[13]

In assembling the Estates-General he believed he could use its power as a means of increasing his own. He built a great cult of his own personal popularity. But there came a time when Necker could not control the conspiracy he had unleashed. Now the conspirators, sure of conquering with the tools obtained from him, abandoned the traitor who had put them in a position of power. That cleared the way for the third faction, the republicans, to seize power.[14]

Ferrand dated the Revolution from the declaration of the Third Estate that it was the National Assembly. At that point there was only one way to stop it, "to dissolve the Estates-General on the spot, to judge and execute the principal rebels: twelve heads would have saved the State." But the government was weak and nothing happened.[15]

Next Ferrand embarked on a discussion of political theory and took up the question of natural rights. He said that if one were referring to a state of nature, as the philosophes were, there was no such thing as natural rights, but only certain mental faculties, which meant that each individual could use his capacities to the best of his ability. Natural rights, on the other hand, involved obligations, connections, and duties, things that could not exist in a state of nature.

He claimed that common sense demonstrated that one could not apply the example of man in a state of nature in regulating the rights of man in society. People in a state of nature could do whatever their natural abilities permitted. But in entering society they renounced this unlimited freedom and took up social intercourse, from which sprang obligations and rights. In a state of nature one had the ability to achieve justice for oneself; in society one renounced it to seek justice from the group.[16]

Moreover he asserted that men were unequal, both in a state of nature and in society. In the former their abilities were unequal; in the latter their situations were different. They were made equal by law, which gave them equal rights to its protection. But this equal protection maintained the inequalities that society had established. On these inequalities liberty was built. Once destroyed, by an equal distribution of property, liberty collapsed at the same time.[17]

Ferrand argued strongly against the concept of popular sovereignty. He said that it would mean a state perpetually in revolution, which is to say a state without a society. The people could not have had sovereignty in a state of nature because they were isolated, and sovereignty involved a connection between a sovereign and his subjects. Since the people had never had sovereignty it would be impossible for them to acquire it. And if they had relinquished it, they would not get it back except by unanimous consent of all the subjects.[18]

He also came out forcefully against the idea of political decentralization and said that France needed a central government because it was made up of a large number of parts, all of which led to the same point. He claimed that they could not be contained except by a strong central force. "To divide that strength would be to destroy its effects and to undermine the structure."[19]

Borrowing a leaf from Edmund Burke, Ferrand argued that each state should work to improve gradually the government it had. This process should be guided by duties, rather than by rights, and should learn from the conflagration that had hit France. And it would involve the destruction forever of the work of the French Revolution, which had upset the tranquility of Europe, disordered France, degraded royalty, brought an end to justice, overthrown morality, frustrated the national will, and ruined religion.[20]

As far as France was concerned, it should return to the constitution of the Old Regime, where he said the monarchy was absolute without being despotic, and where the clergy, the nobility, and the magistrates all had their place. It was necessary only to remember what France was like before the Estates-General and what it had become since. France would never be anything if it was not what it had always been. It should not remain a republic nor become again a constitutional monarchy, nor undergo any change in its government. The only answer was the restoration of the old constitution and the reform of the abuses that had crept into it.[21]

By 1793, Ferrand's argument for the restoration of the old orders was impractical. And his assertion that the abuses of the Old Regime could easily be reformed was not realistic.

Ferrand did recognize the abuses in the government's finances and the indebtedness that stemmed from the French support of the American Revolution, but then went on to say that much of the problem was the fault of financiers and speculators, who were outside the government. When the financial crisis reached its peak he said that the state should have moved "swiftly and decisively," but it did not, and he claimed it was not necessary to assemble either the notables or the Estates-General. A former member of the Parlement, he was able to criticize the Parlement for promoting the Estates-General. Though he lacked any full-blown theory of an aristocratic resurgence, the germ of that idea is present.

Tackling the political thought that lay behind the Revolution, as a good royalist he emphasized duties and obligations, rather than rights, and maintained that there were no rights in a state of nature. He argued against equality, both in a state of nature and in society, in the name of liberty. And he attacked the idea of popular sovereignty on practical and historical grounds.

He took pleasure in using Rousseau to combat the notion of political decentralization, though his comments here were more relevant to the situation in 1791 than in 1793. And he borrowed from Burke to stress the need for gradual change. He concluded that France would be all right if it would only return to the constitution of the Old Regime.

Ferrand deserves credit for recognizing that there were abuses in the Old Regime, though he did not understand the extent or the depth of the problems. He was candid about the role played by Parlement. But then he slipped into a conspiracy theory of history. Everything basically was all right, if only the conspirators had not been present and if there had been good ministers.

Another royalist who published during this period was the abbé Antoine Sabatier (1742–1817), known as de Castres, an opportunist who wrote against the philosophes during the Old Regime, helped found the *Journal Politique-Nationale* in 1789 with Antoine de Rivarol, emigrated after the taking of the Bastille, and in 1793–1794 wrote *Pensées et observations morales et politiques pour servir à la connaissance des vrais principes du gouvernement.*[22]

Sabatier began this work with a discussion of the nature of man. He said that while Hobbes maintained that man was born bad and Rousseau claimed that he was born good, actually he was neither and became one or the other by the force of circumstances. The only sentiment that people had when they came into the world was a love of themselves, a concept he took directly from Rousseau.

He then followed Rousseau's lead and argued that civilized people were much more inclined to evil than people in a state of nature because the more connections man had with his fellow men the more wicked and unhappy he became. In civilized societies each individual achieved his success at the expense of others. Doctors and pharmacists wanted sickness, suppliers desired war, monopolists looked forward to famine, and priests profited from mortality. Civilization thus taught men to hate and to injure each other.

Since primitive man, on the other hand, had a limited number of needs he was sheltered from such passions. He knew nothing about public opinion, which produced the vices that infested society. Men in a state of nature could satisfy their own limited needs themselves, without hurting others, and therefore could usually live in peace. Hence Rousseau was right to praise the life of savages and to flee from urban society.[23]

Sabatier went on to say that man in a state of nature was free of the sin of self-pride, while man in society was riddled with it. He defined self-pride as a feeling that made each individual think only of himself. Natural man, while not perfect, was animated by a healthy love of self that included concern for others and made room for pity, humanity, tenderness, and virtue.[24]

Sabatier continued his discussion of the nature of man by asserting that passions were stronger than reason. Passions, in fact, governed the world. While reason might command, passions only were obeyed. "Reason hides before energetic passions, as a fleeing Slave before an irritated Master, and does not reappear except to flatter him shamefully."[25]

Vices, he went on, were a natural part of civilized society. No government could survive without them. "Take away from men ambition, cupidity, jealousy, hate, fear, superstition, hypocrisy . . . the love of the marvelous and of falsehood, they will stop being sociable; the ties that unite them will be broken, and Society will dissolve."[26] After hunger and thirst, superstitution and fanaticism were the best means to use in leading people. In governing one should not seek to extinguish them, but learn how to use them to best advantage.[27]

Given the depraved condition of civilized people, Christianity was useful and necessary. Without it people would abuse their faculties and become egotistical, hardened, useless, and dependent. In this utilitarian approach kings who wanted their kingdom to last and their subjects to be happy should remember that wise states had always protected religion. And Christianity, which had the best principles and the best morality, was the most appropriate to sustain that feeling of mutual affection between ruler and ruled that would produce the welfare of all. Religion was of such basic importance that, while religion could get along without government, no government could survive without religion.[28]

Sabatier concluded his remarks on religion by arguing for a state religion and for religious intolerance. A state religion, according to him, preserved "order, subordination, strength, union, and tranquility." Therefore, whoever attacked it was an enemy of the state.[29]

It was true that thoughts and opinions should not fall within the jurisdiction of civil law. It should only touch actions. So a person who did not believe in the true religion was someone to complain about, but not to punish. But if that person taught, preached, or wrote about a forbidden religion, then he could be punished, not for his beliefs, but for breaking the law.[30]

Nothing was more dangerous, said Sabatier, than to authorize a second religion when there already was a dominant one. The truth of that assertion, he thought, was amply borne out by the history of Calvinism in France. It "loosened the sacred tie of religion, reduced the number of the faithful, corrupted morality, and eventually led to anarchy and to republicanism."[31]

After coming up with a utilitarian argument for religion, Sabatier then produced a utilitarian rationale for absolute government. He began by asserting that monarchy was the "least vicious and the most favorable to the greatest number of subjects."[32]

He went on to maintain that sovereignty was based on force. It was natural for one man to subjugate other men, he thought, as it was for men to subdue animals. Thus the sovereignty that some men had over whole nations was also reasonable because it went along with human nature. Sovereignty came from "courage, intellect, persuasion, or by the favor of circumstances," and it maintained itself by power or force.[33] With a deep bow to Hobbes and with a great show of realism, Sabatier claimed that all states, past, present, and future, would be established by violence, murder, crime, and treason, and that even the most legitimate authority was based initially on force.[34]

He continued by saying that as men were imperfect, governments were imperfect too. They were established in a rough-and-ready fashion out of necessity and in the midst of disorder, tumult, and murder. Hence they could not help but be affected by their origin. In fact all modern constitutions were defective and carried with them the flaws that would lead to their overthrow. But the least imperfect of the constitutions were the monarchical ones.[35]

Sabatier argued that the more sovereign authority was concentrated the better. Hence a monarchical constitution was better if it concentrated power, and the English constitution, which dispersed authority, was one of the most defective that had ever existed. Hence English kings had to stoop to corruption to accomplish their goals. To limit sovereign power was to paralyze it and to bring about its destruction. In all monarchies strength and prosperity could only come when the kings were absolute and independent.[36]

In another show of realism he also maintained that the interests of the state overrode all other objectives. "Strength, necessity and success legitimate everything in politics." Conservation of the state was the highest priority of states, to which all else was sacrificed: fairness, religion, and honor. Political imperatives were so great that even religion and virtue had to recognize their claims.[37]

Returning to his thoughts on the nature of man, he said that people were so unreasonable that a workable democracy was out of the question. Flattered by those who wanted to make use of them, they became the slaves of their captors. Then their attention was diverted by another faction, they overthrew their former idols, etc. "People were made to be governed and not to have a part in Government." Only men who were ignorant or who wished to mislead could praise democracy.[38]

Not only were the people irrational, they could not be made reasonable. One could write all kinds of moral and political tracts for them, but it would make no difference. They could never grasp anything but their own immediate interests. They were uneducable, and in any case their work would never give them the time to be educated. Anything beyond religious instruction would only make them more anxious and more unhappy. Since even learned men disagreed on important moral and political questions, how could one hope to get an entire nation to agree on what was right and necessary? Only the enemies of the best interests of the people, he concluded, wanted the people to govern.[39]

Sabatier next turned to conventions, and laws and the power of the King with respect to them. He said that the more men reflected on their situation, their needs and their troubles, the more they realized they had to help each other. They then formed conventions that told them what was permitted and forbidden.[40] At the same time he made it very clear that these conventions were the first laws and that there was no such thing as an *a priori* natural law. Rights came from positive laws. If there had been such a thing as natural law it would have been evident, common, universal, and one would have to make an effort to deviate from it, but such was not the case.[41]

Furthermore, as a good conservative he thought there was no universal morality or justice appropriate to all people at all times. Such an idea existed "only in the vaporous brain of the philosophes." Justice and morality always developed within the context of a particular society or community. For example, the vices and virtues of the subjects of an aristocratic republic were not the same as those of a monarchy. Human morality arose from human customs, which varied widely.[42]

He then directed his attention to the relationship between sovereignty and law. According to Sabatier the sovereign was the law, and there could be no other such authority in civil society. The sovereign will had to be free and independent, without any contradiction or obstruction. Otherwise it could not promote the general interest and the common good of the community.

Moreover, sovereignty would not be independent if it were not absolute, beyond any convention, so that it was free to reform the laws and respond to changing circumstances that affected the state. The sovereign made the law, but he should be guided by reason and wisdom, which would help him determine what was best for the preservation and welfare of the state. And it was contradictory and absurd to suppose that the legislative power should be separate from the executive power because the union of these powers was what constituted sovereignty.[43]

He then took up the rights and the responsibilities of the sovereign and of subjects. They were, he maintained, the same as those enumerated in Rousseau's *Social Contract*. The sovereign, from his side, should never impose unnecessary sacrifices on the members of the community, but should always look out for their welfare. But every sovereign had a right to the wealth, the labor, the liberty, even the life of each member of the community because society had as its aim the preservation and the greatest benefit of the people. So the people could have no will but that of the sovereign, who was the only judge of what would help or hinder the community.[44] The sovereign prince could abuse his authority, but in so doing he acted against himself and resembled an individual who cut himself unnecessarily and who, if he repeated the action often enough, would destroy himself.[45]

One could not deny, he admitted, that most governments were established by the force of conquest. Nations, subjected by warriors, were forced to accept the law of the conquerors. The natives, happy to escape with their lives, were willing to give up part of their freedom and their property to the new regime. But if the rights of reason were forgotten during the taking of power, they were not given up. Once in position it was in the interest of the new ruler to dedicate himself to the welfare and prosperity of his new subjects, if only so he could maintain his place and promote his interests. So, in the long run, force and conquest neither bestowed rights nor took them away. Ultimately no ruler could prove stronger than a entire nation, and every ruler had to remember that it was to his advantage to promote the best interests of his country.[46]

In this same area he thundered against the revolutionary concepts of equality and liberty. He said that equality did not exist, either in a state of nature or in society. Once again he maintained that in civilized nations the only determinant of whether something was good or bad was whether it was in the general interest. So if it promoted the general welfare, it was all right to have serfs or slaves. And in any case there were a lot of people worse off than slaves! So much for equality. As far as liberty was concerned, the same principle prevailed: the state limited the freedom of some individuals to preserve the freedom of the greater number, as it sacrificed the lives of some citizens to ensure the safety of the state.[47]

Probably Sabatier's most interesting idea was that the king should control public opinion, something that the French government had failed to do in the period before the French Revolution.[48] It was the writings of Pierre Bayle, Nicolas Freret, Nicolas Boulanger, Voltaire, Rousseau, and the Encyclopedists, according to Sabatier, that undermined respect for religion, morality, and royalty. They were the ones who made people believe that man was born free, that religion and monarchy created slaves, and that sovereignty belonged to the people. As a result the throne was overturned, the monarchy destroyed, and the monarchical spirit extinguished in France.[49] Sabatier said he had warned the ministers of Louis XVI of the philosophic flood that eventually carried away the French monarchy, but to no avail. Now he hoped the German princes would learn this grim lesson. They had to realize that public opinion was more powerful than kings, and that they would be strong only if they controlled it. The masses were essentially ignorant and credulous. To dominate them rulers either had to control the writers or to enforce a complete silence, which was almost impossible.[50]

Sabatier steadfastly opposed freedom of the press. He said that the only one who had the right to speak to the public was the government because it alone was responsible for maintaining order and guarding against vice and error. Preachers and judges[51] were simply the agents of the government. Authors should be allowed to publish only if they obtained the permission of the state; there was no right to publish.[52]

In the meantime, the state should keep a careful eye on literature, which could undermine it. Literature had always had a great influence over the spirit and the morals of nations, over revolutions, and often was the cause of revolutions. To think of it only as a source of glory and diversion was to miss the point that it was subject to abuse and degradation. From the corruption of taste came the corruption of morality and eventually the ruin of the state itself.[53]

What the government should do was to encourage right-thinking writers.[54] To a rebellious and ambitious state of mind one should oppose calm and well-ordered reflections that would lead people back to order. To restrain the spirit of independence that had been introduced into literature, one should arm writers who were ready to remind people of the rules and to point out the abuses. Newspapers directed by loyal and skillful writers could offer a sure means to put down insurrections, to establish good beliefs, and to align public opinion with the position of the government.[55] As far as books were concerned, he claimed that one could inscribe on the doors of all the large libraries: "poisons for the spirit and the heart." Like drugs, they did more harm than good to people who used them. Both caused users to deteriorate, rather than to get stronger, and were only useful as antidotes and sleeping pills. But, since there was a felt need for books, what one had to do was avoid the bad books and read only the good ones.[56]

As far as the fine arts were concerned,[57] they were useless in supporting empires or in promoting the happiness of people. They led people away from social virtue. A person trained to exercise his imaginaton was naturally inclined toward freedom and independence, which made it difficult for him to give way before the duties of society and the sacrifices that the general welfare demanded.[58]

After these suggestions to the German princes, Sabatier concluded with the causes of the French Revolution. Here he was a forerunner of the aristocratic resurgence theory.[59] He pointed his finger especially at the Ordinance of 1781, which excluded non-nobles from the officer ranks in the army. Sabatier, who had argued earlier against equality, now maintained that every citizen was entitled to serve his country according to his talents. He found the Ordinance of 1781 opposed to the national interest, to reason, and to the natural order. And the parlements were also moving to exclude non-nobles from their ranks. He considered such moves a conspiracy against the rest of the citizens. It was no wonder, he observed, that the Third Estate became agitated against the government and against the nobility. Furthermore, the nobles should have paid as much taxes as anyone else.[60] It was the division and the weakening of royal authority, he went on, that led to the fall of the monarchy. The parlements disobeyed the king. Their vetoes contributed more to the overthrow of the monarchy than did the financial crisis.[61]

Then he came up with a conspiracy theory: if Louis XVI, at the urging of Necker, had not permitted Protestants to attend the Estates-General he would not have been killed. It was the Calvinist Barnave, with his seditious speeches, who corrupted the first assembly. And it was the intrigues of the Calvinist Minister Rabaud Saint-Etienne, member of both the National Assembly and the Convention, that contributed to the complete extinction of royalty and the establishment of a French Republic.[62]

Finally he came to the organic theory of history, which he had picked up from Burke and from other French conservatives. Changes, Sabatier thought, were always dangerous in monarchical states. Any custom, useful or not, was a link in the chain of the political machine. In making changes one should imitate the slowness of the changes that took place in the course of nature. Such deliberation prevented abuses and thoughtless innovation. In politics, as in medicine, it was easier to prevent sickness than to heal. This did not mean that one should do nothing, especially in cases of decay, but one should proceed with extreme care, and only when assured that an alteration would not produce a dangerous shock.[63]

Sabatier was not original, and he was not always consistent. But he is interesting as an indefatigable collector of ideas and as one who had something important to say about the force of public opinion. His comments on the nature of man show the influence of Hobbes and of Rousseau. Following in Rousseau's footsteps, he sought to give more currency to the notion that savages were noble and civilized men corrupt. This was a useful base, of course, for his advocacy of absolute government. And he promoted the idea that men could be governed by their vices, which authoritarian governments have been only too willing to do since his time. Furthermore he took a common conservative tack in justifying Christianity, not for its own sake, but primarily as a means to promote social order. This led him to advocate a state religion and religious intolerance. Sabatier sounds tough: men are selfish and evil, and hence governments had to be strong. But then in developing his position he undoubtedly relied on the utilitarian approach of Voltaire and others, and he made frequent references to the general welfare. So he ends up sounding something like a pussycat.

In his discussion of law and the power of the king, he had a problem that he did not resolve: when talking about the formation of conventions and laws he verged on a contract theory, but he still tried to deny the contract theory of government.[64] His discussion of the coming of the French Revolution is sketchy, but with his sponge-like mind he picked up two ideas that have had great influence in modern historiography: the aristocratic resurgence of the eighteenth century and the organic theory of history. However he deserves to be remembered primarily because of his discussion of the force of public opinion. Though his ideas started with a simplistic conspiracy theory of history—the French Revolution was the fault of the Protestants—and he clearly overestimated the impact of ideas in history, in part to enhance his importance as a manipulator of public opinion, he did point his finger at a failure of the Old Regime and thereby helped set an ideological agenda for authoritarian governments in the future.

Both Ferrand and Sabatier took up the causes of the French Revolution and general questions of political thought, though Ferrand devoted more time to the former and Sabatier to the latter. With Ferrand, who clearly did not recognize that any fundamental or irrevocable changes had taken place, it was almost as if one could snap one's fingers and the old orders would return, the King would correct a few minor flaws, and all would be well. His account denied reality or ignored it.

Ferrand embarked on a detailed analysis of the causes of the Revolution. He kept blaming a lack of leadership, but he never pointed to the King, which he probably felt he could not do when he was serving the King's brother and when Louis XVI had become a martyr. So, as often in earlier royalist accounts, it was the fault of the ministers, the philosophes, the speculators, and the Protestants. Necker, a frequent royalist villain, merited special attention. This part of his analysis has little that is original; one in fact could call it warmed-up royalist propaganda. Ferrand then rounded off his account by making the simplistic argument that in mid-June 1789 the King could easily have dissolved the Estates-General.

The most interesting arguments Ferrand advances on this subject are his admission that the government had financial problems, though he related them to the interests of the speculators, and the notion, coming from a former member of Parlement, that the Parlement's support for the Estates-General contributed to the coming of the Revolution.

Though Sabatier spent much less time on the causes of the Revolution, he did not get so caught up in surface events. It is true that he also pointed the finger of blame at the Protestants, but then directed our attention to more fundamental matters: the aristocratic resurgence and the need for gradual change.

Ferrand, in his relatively brief remarks on political thought, took the usual conservative position that there were no natural rights in a state of nature. The emphasis is on duties, not rights. He also took the familiar stands for inequality, against popular sovereignty, against decentralization, and for gradual change.

Though Sabatier was not original, he had more to say about political thought and said it more persuasively. For example, he didn't say people were good or bad by nature but by circumstance, which shows the impact of the Enlightenment. Similarly he may have taken the notion that civilized people were worse than uncivilized direct from Rousseau. But then he filtered these ideas through a conservative framework, arguing that passions were stronger than reason and that government should make use of the vices present in civilized society.

Sabatier saw religion and politics as indispensable to each other. But he had trouble making up his mind about sovereignty. On the one hand, he said it was based on force and should be as concentrated as possible; he thought the interests of the state were paramount. He believed people were irrational. He came out against natural law, against both equality and liberty, and for absolute government.

But then he tried to use utilitarian arguments, not always successfully, to defend his position. He claimed, without proof, that monarchy was the "least vicious and most favorable to the greatest number." He maintained that rights came from conventions, not from natural rights, and then sought to deny the contract theory of government. And he borrowed from Rousseau to argue that the sovereign should look out for the welfare of his subjects. This utilitarian approach could be dangerous to royalists. What if people concluded, as many did during the French Revolution, that kings like Louis XIV, Louis XV, and Louis XVI had not promoted the best interests of the people?

But he was right in insisting that kings needed to control public opinion, and that the French monarchy fell partly because it failed to do so. Though he had the benefit of hindsight, in an age of democratic revolution it was no longer enough to cite the divine rights of kings and expect everyone to fall pasively into line. His understanding of the force of public opinion led him to urge governments to encourage dependable authors, and it also meant he would have curbed freedom of the press, looked on literature as suspect, and discouraged any unfettered play of the fine arts.

Did they have a program for France in 1793? I think not. For one thing both emigrated in 1789, and they did not demonstrate much understanding of what had gone on after that. Both, playing for influence in émigrés circles, were pretty much caught up in a hermetically sealed world. This vision especially comes out in Ferrand's simplistic account of the causes of the Revolution. In his political thought Ferrand again relied on the old royalist shibboleths. Sabatier, on the other hand, reached out for ideas wherever he could find them, but sometimes when trying to fit new ideas into an old armature he fell into contradiction. Even then his attempts could be instructive.

NOTES

A version of this chapter was delivered at the Society for French Historical Studies at Columbia, South Carolina, on March 19, 1988.

1. By 1793 he had abandoned his former position of championing the aristocratic resurgence and become an advocate of absolutism. *Nouvelle Biographie Générale*, 17 (1856), col. 493; Antoine François Claude, comte de Ferrand, *Mémoires du comte Ferrand, Ministre d'état sous Louis XVIII* (Paris, 1897), viii–ix.

2. Antoine François Claude, comte de Ferrand, *Le Rétablissement de la monarchie* (n.p., September 1793), 6–8.

3. Ibid., 11.

4. Ibid., 12–13.

5. Ibid., 11–12

6. Ibid., 14–15.

7. Ibid., 17.

8. Ibid., 18–19, 21.

9. Ibid., 21.

10. Ibid., 22–24.

11. Ibid., 34–35.

12. Ibid., 39.

13. Ibid., 40–43.

14. Ibid., 45–47, 54–55.

15. Ibid., 55–56.

16. Ibid., 93–95.

17. Ibid., 96.

18. Ibid., 101–2, 104–5; Paul H. Beik, *The French Revolution Seen from the Right: Social Theories in Motion, 1789–1799* (Philadelphia, 1956), 54.

19. Ferrand, *Le Rétablissement de la monarchie*, 132.

20. *Le Rétablissement de la monarchie*, 185.

21. Ibid., 196, 217–20.

22. Beik, *The French Revolution Seen from the Right*, 60; *Nouvelle Biographie Générale*, 42 (1863), cols. 958–62.

23. Antoine Sabatier, *Pensées et observations morales et politique pour servir à la connaissance des vrais principes du governement* (Vienna, 1794) 18, 21, 23–24.

24. Ibid., 24–25.
25. Ibid., 53.
26. Ibid., 61.
27. Ibid., 70.
28. Ibid., 90–91, 162.
29. Ibid., 160.
30. Ibid., 131.
31. Ibid., 131, 133.
32. Ibid., 4.
33. Ibid., 379–380.
34. Ibid., 388. Although he did not give him credit, Sabatier probably borrowed from Simon Linguet's *Théorie des lois civiles* and other writings. See Simon Nicolas Henry Linguet, *Théorie des loix civiles, ou Principes fondamentaux de la société* (London, 1767), I, 73–76, 82–83, and Darlene Gay Levy, *The Ideas and Careers of Simon-Nicolas-Henri Linguet, A Study in Eighteenth-Century French Politics* (Urbana, 1980), 84–110. I am indebted to Jeremy Popkin for this suggestion.
35. Ibid., 411–12.
36. Ibid., 436–38.
37. Ibid., 388–89.
38. Ibid., 432.
39. Ibid., 432–33.
40. Ibid., 406.
41. Ibid., 36.
42. Ibid., 389–90.
43. Ibid., 426–29. Sabatier changed his opinion from time to time, but on this subject he seems to have been consistent. See his pamphlet, *La Vérité vengée* (Liège, 1789) 32: "Sovereignty is one, indivisible. It would be divided and void if the laws of the Sovereign were submitted to a tribunal. When the will of the King is no longer the supreme will, when obedience is conditioned and when the situation depends on those who almost always have an interest in contradicting it, then there no longer is a monarchy."
44. To support this proposition he quoted Rousseau's *Social Contract*, Book II, Chapter 5: "He who wishes to save his life at the expense of others should also give it for others, when it is necessary . . . and when the Prince says to the citizen, it is expected that you die, he should die."
45. *Pensées et observations morales et politiques*, 430–32.
46. Ibid., 410–11.
47. Ibid., 39, 44–45.
48. This was not an original idea with Sabatier, but one he developed considerably. For earlier references, see the statement by Anoine Rivarol, Sabatier's former colleague, in the *Journal Politique-National*, I, no. 13, August 9, 1789, 4–5, and by Antoine Rivarol's brother, Claude François Rivarol, in the *Journal-Pie*, January 28, 1792. It is of course implicit in the conspiracy theory of history, which French conservatives made great use of in explaining the French Revolution. This idea received new currency from R.R. Palmer, *The Age of Democratic Revolution*, I (Princeton, 1959), 86–89, where he talked about a failure of public relations. For Napoleon's propaganda skills, see Robert Holtman, *The Napoleonic Revolution*, (Philadelphia and New York, 1967), 63–64.
49. *Pensées et observations morales et politiques*, 170–71.

50. Ibid., 416. If the German princes were seriously interested in pursuing their problem, he offered to write them a manual of less than six pages about how to do it. Ibid., 417. He was obviously fishing for their patronage.

51. With perhaps a thought here to the remonstrances of the parlements. See Palmer, *The Age of Democratic Revolution.*

52. Ibid., 153.

53. Ibid., 163–64.

54. Among whom Sabatier would name himself.

55. Ibid., 169–70.

56. Ibid., 212–13.

57. Here he included eloquence, poetry, painting, sculpture, declamation, music, pantomine, and dance.

58. Ibid., 199–202, 209.

59. Earlier formulations of this idea include Gabriel Sénac de Meilhan's *Des Principes et des Causes de la Révolution en France*, (London, 1790), 78–79 and Claude François Rivarol's *Journal-Pie*, January 22, 1792.

60. *Pensées et observations*, 453–54.

61. Ibid., 443–44.

62. Ibid., 156. This of course reinforces his earlier remarks against religious toleration.

63. Ibid., 469.

64. The contract theory of government was also implicit in his assertion that governments had to follow the general interests of the people or they would be overthrown. For his dilemma here, see Beik, *The French Revolution Seen from the Right*, 61–62.

CHAPTER V

French Royalism During Thermidor and the Directory

During Thermidor and the first part of the Directory, French royalist writers had their best chance yet to explain what had gone wrong during the Old Regime, why the French Revolution had come into power and been able to succeed, and why they thought it would be better to replace it and restore the monarchy. The Terror was over and a transition was taking place. This chapter will examine what the royalists made of their opportunities.

Focusing first on the explanations of the causes of the Revolution and why it succeeded, we begin with Antoine François Claude, comte de Ferrand, who had first championed absolutism in his *Le Rétablissement de la monarchie*, published in 1793.[1] In 1795 he returned with *Des Causes qui ont empêché la contre-révolution en France*. In explaining why the Revolution was able to succeed, he was franker about Louis XVI's role than before. Now he depicted Louis XVI as so weak that he abandoned his strongest allies because he lacked confidence in his own judgment. He also had a misguided sense of compassion; instead of punishing a guilty person, he thought only of the blood of a subject that would be shed. Hence he failed to realize that strong and legitimate measures would re-establish principles that had become unsettled. Thus, as a prince he was indecisive and weak.[2]

But the chief villain, as in his earlier account, was Necker, who encouraged the weaknesses of Louis XVI as a means to accomplish his own objectives.[3] The weakness of Louis XVI and the treachery of his ministers put the state at the mercy of the political factions, who made use of the Enlightenment to mislead the people by extinguishing the torch of religion—the only reliable support of monarchy.[4] All of this was a review of his earlier argument.

The French Revolution was also able to succeed, he now believed, because the foreign powers had not struck against it at the decisive moment. They should have moved immediately after the night of October 5–6. Instead they carried on as before, and let the King be taken to Paris and become the puppet of the revolutionaries.[5]

After listening to a bewildering series of conflicting counsels in 1790–1791 and, as a result, falling into his usual indecisiveness, in June of 1791 Louis XVI at last took action and attempted to flee. Even though he was caught and brought back to Paris, there was still time to save the monarchy if the Holy Roman Emperor had been willing to act, but he was not.

Louis XVI then let himself be convinced that even though the Constitution of 1791 was bad, the people thought it was good and would not be persuaded otherwise except by experience. Louis, not wanting to shed blood unnecessarily and always interested only in the welfare of his subjects, agreed to sanction the Constitution.[6]

So, Ferrand said, the French Revolution succeeded because of the weakness of Louis XVI, the machinations of Necker and other advisers, the effects of the Enlightenment, and the failure of foreign kings to defend Louis XVI. All this led, of course, to the fall of the monarchy in August of 1792. It also resulted in the overthrow of the Constitution of 1791, which was replaced by a society based on blood, called the French Republic, dedicated to the overthrow of all society.[7]

Also during the period of the Thermidorean Reaction, the royalist newspaper *La Quotidienne*[8] undertook a review of the causes of the Revolution. In an article dated August 27, 1795, the author was clearly hostile to the role played by the court of Louis XVI. Specifically the author blamed Loménie de Brienne, whom he accused of preferring to fight a dangerous game against the parlements rather than waging war, as he should have, against the press. But at the same time the parlements were faulted for being willing to perish with the government, as long as they had a chance to attack the monarchy.

Another cause cited was overpopulation. Everything tended to go well as long as there was more work than workers. But when there was a lack of jobs, as there was on the eve of the Revolution, the result was unemployed, and therefore dangerous, men. In that case, one should have promoted emigration and established colonies or set up a strong constitution to keep the people in check. But instead Louis XVI assembled the people so they could write their own constitution; then the troublemakers took over and all was lost.

La Quotidienne concluded by suggesting that the Revolution was really a war of the have-nots against the haves. A symptom of the problem was that the Queen, in loading a few individuals with favors, alienated many of the nobility and the clergy. These people, assembled in the parlements, were then both the instigators of the Revolution and its first victims. So we have another account that describes the role of the privileged and suggests an aristocratic revolution against them. They became victims because the rest of the population moved to attack their privileges. Soon those who had nothing were attacking all those who had property, and there was nothing to stop them.[9]

The final conservative spokesman during the Thermidorean period was Jean Thomas Langlois (1747–1804), a lawyer whose pamphlets were cited prominently in the right-wing press of the time.[10] He began the first of these, *Des*

Gouvernemens qui ne conviennent pas à la France, in 1795, with a blast at the philosophes. What monster, he asked, had produced the devouring lava of the French Revolution? Modern philosophy. While detaching people from their loyalty to the state and pretending to carry them to a heavenly realm of superior intelligence, it was really reducing them to a level below the savages.[11]

Sometimes, however, royalists were able to overcome their fixation on the past and to elaborate reasons why and how one should restore the monarchy. Certainly the Terror offered them a powerful argument against the Revolution and its breakdown an opportunity to state their case.

Ferrand claimed that in destroying the divine right of kings, as well as the existing natural and political laws, the Revolution destroyed the social ties that held society together. There was then nothing to replace them with, no matter how hard one tried.[12]

He then explicitly linked the fate of the French monarchy with monarchy throughout Europe: "if royalty is not re-established in *France*, all the States are destroyed."[13] He then argued that one could not overthrow the conspiracy against the thrones of Europe except by attacking its source in France. There the Jacobins prepared their grand designs for Europe. Currently they were occupied with the war, but as soon as they had concluded it to their satisfaction they would call upon the dregs of society to overthrow the states of Europe. And there could be no coexistence with the Revolution. If one did not destroy it, one recognized it. By recognizing it one encouraged people to imitate it. And, if the Revolution was approved and successful, there was no doubt that other people would follow its example.[14]

Actually the French people liked their kings. But in a giddy moment, led astray by political factions and by the weakness of the ministers, the people had been swept away so quickly they didn't know what was happening. But by 1795 they understood their situation, and they bore the pain of their revolt. After a great deal of madness and crime they found themselves trapped between silence and the guillotine. "A people among whom the tyrants choose or take each day by chance a hundred heads cannot remain voluntarily in that condition; one must help them to escape."[15] And the powers should announce their intentions by recognizing Louis XVIII as the King and the rightful ruler of France.

The states should draw up a clear declaration in which they denounced the social revolution and formally recognized the King of France. Otherwise the revolution would continue to spread in Europe and menace every government. One should move with all available force to crush the Revolution, including mobilizing all the counter-revolutionary forces under Louis XVIII.[16]

Ferrand concluded by emphasizing again that peace with the French Revolution was impossible. It did not want concessions or submissions; it wanted to totally annihilate its opposition. So either the Revolution would triumph completely, or the kings would have to destroy the Revolution.[17]

Another defense of the royalist position came from Gabriel Sénac de Meilhan (1736–1803), a former intendant under the Old Regime, in his 1795 *Du gouvernement, des moeurs, et des conditions en France, avant la révolution*. Sénac made it clear that he supported the position of Du Bos that the nobles were dependent for their position on the king.[18] At the same time he maintained that France had a constitutional tradition that limited the power of the king. "The regulations made by the Estates-General, the principles and maxims adopted by these assemblies, the collection of the Laws registered in the Parlements, and the right of remonstrance were a brake on arbitrary authority."[19]

Sénac did recognize that the parlements were sometimes more interested in fighting for their authority and for their prerogatives than in pursuing the interests of the people. But the time had come to make changes, the chief of which was to establish a system of taxation that was fairer and less complicated. The Parlements would have offered opposition, but a government that was "firm, economical, and enlightened" would have overcome these obstacles, rallied support, and eventually enlisted the help of the parlements themselves.[20]

Even though he was very willing to point out its flaws, in the final analysis Sénac offered a defense of the French monarchy. While admitting that some monarchs were better than others, he asserted: "the calm, that a well-established royalty makes prevail in a large country, is one of the greatest advantages of monarchical Government. Royal power is a rock, against which are broken without noise the impetuous waves of ambition and as a result calm is established in all parts."[21]

Jean Langlois also turned his attention to constitutional questions and argued that a large country with a large population and a lot of resources, which bordered on states of equal power, should have an absolute monarchy. Such states had to cope with great distances and with the possibility of sudden invasions from neighboring countries. In such a situation whoever governed had to have great power in order to mount an effective defense. Most of the countries that surrounded France had this capability and France did too before the Revolution of 1789.[22]

Langlois then went on to attack the separation of power between an executive and a legislative branch. He claimed that the division of powers would lead first to civil war, then to anarchy, and finally to the dissolution of all government. Two powers in a state inevitably would become rivals. Either the legislative power would mobilize public opinion and crush the executive power, or the executive would make itself the master and the legislative power would be eliminated. "In the first case you would have the tyranny of 700 to 800 despots; in the second you would have the despotism of one tyrant alone."[23]

The system wouldn't work even if each branch stopped trying to dominate. They would always be working at cross purposes because of differences of opinion. Unable to agree, they never would be able to accomplish anything. The eventual result would either be constant change, which would overthrow the fortunes of families and the lives of individuals, or such a fear of instability that the choice would be to let the state stagnate.

But even more serious, according to Langlois, was the ferment that would be produced within the population as a whole. The constant changes would give rise to a number of different political factions, who would play upon popular feelings that any check the government attempted to impose upon the people was a threat to popular sovereignty. How then could the executive branch handle sedition? It would have to turn to the legislative branch, which would waste precious time in discussion. In the meantime the rebels would profit from the delay, from the great distances, and from the large population to assemble a substantial force and mount a powerful resistance.

But it would be even worse if the factions had penetrated the legislative body or the executive council or both. Then the rebel leaders could prolong delays, retard attacks, and ruin all the government's plans. They could even tell the rebels when and where they would be attacked! The rebels would thus possess all the advantages. It would be even worse if the factions were allied with foreign powers. Then the government would inevitably fall.

So, Langlois concluded, the separation of the legislative and the executive powers was absolutely incompatible with the necessities of government in France. Separation would result in rivalries that would weaken it, open the doors to disorganization and anarchy, and plunge the state into either civil war or dissolution. Then either foreign powers would profit from the disarray to invade and dismember France, or one of the branches would destroy the other branch and establish a despotism.[24]

Langlois also argued that a legislature divided into two bodies, with a separate executive power, which was the plan for the constitution of the Directory, would not work in France. He maintained that the requirement for members of the two chambers to be property holders would excite the jealousy of the rest of the nation and plant the seeds of civil war, though why both houses had to be filled with property holders remains unclear.[25]

Langlois furthermore found the system of temporary office-holding in a representative government inappropriate for France. It would never produce good office-holders because the great difficulty of getting into office and the uncertainty about remaining there would discourage good candidates. Those who were smart would spend their time building up their fortune so they could benefit their family and friends. This system, bad enough in times of peace and tranquility, was even worse in periods of adversity. Then there would be a complete lack of preparation and continuity, and there would be one upheaval after another.[26]

Finally he got to the kind of government that was appropriate for France; namely, a monarchy. The French, he said, were an ancient people, who were corrupt, numerous, and living on a continent where monarchy was in the air and had been for fourteen centuries.

If the monarch met with resistance on his return to France, in a replay of the Brunswick Manifesto, Langlois predicted an awful fate for the resisters. Calling upon the international solidarity of kings, as had Ferrand, Langlois predicted that neighboring monarchs would help him, and the republicans would be overcome without any chance of regaining power. The former government would be dissolved, the republicans destroyed, and a hereditary dynasty established.[27]

Langlois issued another pamphlet in the same year, *Qu'est-ce qu'une Convention nationale?* In it he asserted that a nation did not have the right to change its government, and that a convention had even less right to do so than anyone else.[28]

He also argued for elitism: "the will, the discontent of the multitude should not count for anything because in general the blind and ignorant multitude is often satisfied without knowing why. The voice of the smallest number should have here the preponderance because the smallest number in a nation is always the most educated and the most enlightened."[29]

These statements led him to maintain that constitutional change could only come slowly. A constitution, he claimed, was not the work of a year or even a century. It was the product of experience, of the wisdom of many centuries. If one were starting afresh, it would take many unhappy generations before any new constitution could reach a satisfactory state.[30]

Langlois produced one more pamphlet during this period, *De la Souveraineté*, in 1797. He defined sovereignty as the right to make laws and to execute them. In the course of this discussion, in line with his previous ideas, he came out strongly against the idea of popular sovereignty. Such a theory he thought ran counter to all experience and to all reasonable expectations of humanity. In fact he was not able to find a single time in history when the people had been sovereign.[31]

During the Thermidorean period royalists offered both old and new explanations of the causes of the Revolution and of its success. Ferrand drew on the old royalist arsenal to single out Necker as responsible. And he presented the warmed-over explanation that the Revolution was the fault of the political factions, who drew on the ideas of the Enlightenment. But he also assigned more responsibility to Louis XVI than royalists usually had done. Perhaps this was because Louis XVI was no longer in danger, as he was until January of 1793, because the halo of his martyrdom had begun to fade slightly by 1795, and because Louis XVI no longer provided a relevant model. If royalists were going to regain power, and some of them thought there was a chance at this time, leadership was crucial, and the example of Louis XVI did not fit the bill. The other new emphasis in Ferrand's account was that the Old Regime fell and the Revolution succeeded because foreign powers did not help French monarchists. The contemporary message was clear: help restore kingship to France now!

The newspaper *La Quotidienne* also offered a mixture of old and new ideas on this subject. It singled out the court of Louis XVI and the parlements, both well-established ideas by this time. Its depiction of social causes, however, was uncommon in royalist circles. The notion of overpopulation and its effects, with which current demographers would agree, brings in a whole new dimension. And the characterization of the French Revolution as a revolt against privilege has a modern ring to it, one not usually found among the royalists.

On political questions in general, Ferrand has little new to contribute, but he did give an indication of monarchist thinking. The suggestion that the Revolution destroyed ties that bound society together is a version of the organic theory of history, one that can be traced as far back as the hierarchical society of the Middle Ages. His previous explanation that the Revolution succeeded because foreign monarchs failed to help a beleaguered French regime now became a contemporary call for action since all of Europe was threatened by the Jacobins. And there was no room for compromise: either the Revolution would triumph throughout Europe or monarchy would prevail everwhere. The spirit of the Brunswick Manifesto lived on.

Gabriel Sénac de Meilhan's tone, on the other hand, was more moderate. There were constitutional limits on the power of the king—the king was no despot. And yes, the parlements, by opposing needed tax reform, had caused problems in the past, but the government could have put it through nevertheless. Finally he defended monarchy as the best form of rulership for large countries. Though he is not explicit, the implication is that with a strong king, France could have avoided the instability and the chaos of the revolutionary period.

Jean Langlois added to the argument that large countries need strong governments. But then he came up with an incredible assessment of the dangers of limited constitutional government in general and of the separation of powers in particular. He had no appreciation of the possibilities of representative government, and of governing with political differences and with different political parties. The most one can say is that he demonstrated French political inexperience. Langlois was an elitist who denied popular sovereignty, and used tradition and the organic theory of history to contend that change should only came gradually. And, since things had gotten out of line, he repeated the call for international solidarity against the republicans.

In the period of the Directory two writings appeared by Montjoie (Christophe Félix Louis Ventre de la Touloubre, 1746–1816), who had edited a version of the royalist newspaper, *L'Ami du Roi*, from 1790–1792. The first, *Éloge historique et funèbre de Louis XVIe*, was written between January and March of 1793, and published in 1796. It concentrated on the causes of the Revolution and blamed it in part on hate: the hate of the Hapsburgs against the Bourbons, of the Calvinists against the descendants of Louis XIV, of the philosophes against authority, of the Jansenists against the Jesuits, of the duc d'Orléans against his cousin, of the Third Estate against the other two orders, and the hate of one political faction against another.[32]

Another cause Montjoie cited was overpopulation. As a result there were frequent famines, and desperate men roamed the country, ready to commit violence when they could not find food. And the government really did not know what was going on. So Louis XVI had the misfortune to come to power at the wrong time, when it was impossible to lower prices, when he could never give his people anything beyond empty promises, when the population and the number of needy people kept increasing because the Church had fallen into disfavor, and because peace continued to reign.[33]

Given these conditions it was the encyclopedists and the physiocrats whom Montjoie held responsible for the loss of Louis XVI's throne and his head. The former, disciples of Pierre Bayle, armed against him all the sects in the country, corrupted morals, and encouraged the people to commit every excess. The physiocrats mixed up all the economic and political ideas of the day. Their fantasies about political economy and their unfortunate intervention with administrators led to a increase in the scarcity of grain, a raise in prices, the establishment of monopolies, and an increase in discontent and agitation. They finally produced such a state of despair that the people revolted on July 14.[34]

In his explanation of the coming of the French Revolution Montjoie also discussed the financial problems of the Old Regime, which eventually led to the calling of the Estates-General, though he claimed that Louis XVI did everything he could to avert the crisis. When Louis XVI came to the throne he found a large and pressing debt. As a result investors were worried about their capital, and the economic signs were discouraging throughout the country. According to Montjoie what Louis XVI decided to do was to eliminate the deficit by cutting back on his own expenses and on those of the court.[35]

Unfortunately French support for the American Revolution undermined the King's efforts at economy and led to serious financial problems. But the situation was made much worse because Louis XVI was forced by public opinion to name Necker as his Finance Minister. Necker was more a speculator than a statesman and more presumptuous than able. Since he then could not raise taxes to support the American Revolution, he sought refuge in the greed of the capitalists and borrowed as much money from them as he could. As a result the state had to pay back a thousand times more than it could assess in taxation. Also Louis XVI now could not possibly balance expenses with receipts and was forced into a financial labyrinth that no one could escape.[36]

Furthermore, at the beginning of his reign, having the highest opinion of his subjects and not wanting to do anything that wasn't agreeable to them, Louis XVI paid a great deal of attention to their wishes. He believed that public opinion would never mislead him; he followed it in the choice of his ministers and in all other important decisions.

At first this method seemed to work. He dismissed the ministers of Louis XV because they seemed so unpopular that they could no longer accomplish anything. By the same token it seemed necessary to recall the parlements, not only because the courts that had replaced them were so unpopular, but also because the parlements seemed to be oracles of justice who stood as barriers against despotism and license. These two actions brought the King public confidence and affection. From his point of view he could not have begun his reign with more success.[37]

But under Turgot and then under Necker things began to turn sour. Turgot was a physiocrat; Necker "the spoiled child of modern philosophy." Both were opposed to Catholicism, and both were inspired by the philosophes. Both hated France's old constitution and its parlements, and both hungered for new things. The first insurrections broke out under Turgot. Under Necker they grew more serious.[38]

No sooner had the public raised up one idol than it wanted to replace him with another. Finally Louis XVI realized that public opinion had deceived him and that to remain true to his conscience he had to make his own choices. At last he realized that the mass of the nation was corrupt and that if one followed its wishes one would only increase the contagion. But unfortunately time had run out: "the ship of state found itself thrown onto the middle of the rocks; it had to perish and its pilot be drowned." But posterity would judge Louis XVI kindly. It would blame those around him for the errors and the disasters of his reign, and would describe him as "an angel of peace in the midst of the wicked." His only fault was to judge others by himself.[39]

Once the Estates-General was summoned all was lost, though this was not the fault of those who called for it nor of the King who agreed, but only of those who took advantage of the opportunity. From that moment on an interregnum began, that ended with the overthrow of the monarchy.[40]

Montjoie returned to the subject of the causes of the Revolution in his *Histoire de la révolution de France* of 1797 and came up with some additional factors. Now the first cause was Louis XV, who meant well and had able ministers, but unfortunately the guiding principles of the reign were unstable. Also there were long and costly wars, and unfortunate financial operations.[41] These developments alarmed government creditors and prepared the way for all the financial problems of the future.[42]

Another cause that dated from the reign of Louis XV was the writings of the philosophes. Usually, according to Montjoie, the only things necessary to keep the people in check were gold and soldiers. With them most thrones were unshakable and easily able to withstand the blasphemies of impiety and license. But what use were gold and soldiers against opinion? Writers formed public opinion, and kings should keep a very careful watch on them. In the writings of the philosophes, however, the throne wasn't respected any more than the altar. These writers tried to remove all the checks on the people, to destroy all the holy and necessary authorities, and break all the social conventions. The main cause of the Revolution was that the government stood by and let the philosophes disseminate their poison.[43]

Calvinism was another cause of the Revolution. The proof was that Calvinists always behaved the same way that revolutionaries were now behaving. And the principles that were established for the National Assembly came at least in part from Calvinism. Calvinists always aimed to destroy the monarchy, they prepared for it, and those who were imbued with republican ideas could not fail to carry them out.[44]

Finally he cited Loménie de Brienne. Montjoie argued that no one had more of a claim to be the author of the Revolution. Though he was infamous in his own order, he was praised by the philosophes and by some of the courtesans. The higher he rose, the smaller he appeared. The only thing he knew how to do was to parrot the mistakes of Calonne. Although he carried himself like Richelieu, he hadn't the foggiest notion of how to govern. "He compromised the authority of his king, irritated the first prince of the blood, overthrew the parlements, offended all the corps, menaced all fortunes, which is to say that to procure gold for himself he dried up all the sources that could provide it to him."[45]

The next royalist was Antoine François Bertrand de Moleville (1744–1818), who began his career as a member of the parlement at Toulouse and served as intendant of Brittany between 1784 and 1788. After a brief tenure as Minister of Marine in late 1791 and early 1792, he aided the King in various unofficial capacities until August 10, after which Bertrand de Moleville went into exile in England, where he devoted himself to explanations of the French Revolution.[46]

In 1797 Bertrand de Moleville published one of his major works, *Private Memoirs Relative to the Last Year of the Reign of Lewis the Sixteenth*, which was issued in French at the same time and appeared in a second edition in 1816.[47] He supplemented these with his extensive *Annals of the French Revolution*.[48]

He touched on the subject of the coming of the French Revolution in a general fashion in his *Annals* of 1800 and laid the blame clearly on the weakness of the monarchy. It came about because of the "weakness, ignorance, negligence, and numberless errors in the Government." Although it might have been a mistake to convene the Estates-General, its sessions could have been useful if the limits of its authority had been clearly marked out, but that did not happen.[49]

On the same subject he maintained that the early years of the reign of Louis XVI were a time of unrest because the price of wheat was high. But all the government did was to make statements, and the uprisings, which went unpunished, increased. He also mentioned the pernicious example of the American Revolution, the unfortunate borrowing by Necker to support it, the opposition of the parlements to an increase in taxes, the resistance of the Assembly of Notables, the calling of the Estates-General, and the pamphlets and cahiers that accompanied it.[50]

Then he got down to specifics and singled out the philosophes as a contributing factor, though not a basic cause. Under Louis XV the so-called philosophers "created a new power, which they called Public Opinion, and of which they constituted themselves the organs. Its seat existed no where, its Decrees were promulgated only by seditious writings and insolent declamations, which far from expressing the general sentiment or wish, were found, on examination to contain merely the opinions that some pseudo-philosophers took it into their heads to publish."[51] They attacked the throne, the altar, morality, hierarchical society, and all that was most sacred. They called all the authorities before them and pronounced sentence on them. They were bad under Louis XV and became worse under Louis XVI.

But his most thorough-going treatment of the coming of the Revolution appeared in his *Private Memoirs*. There he returned to the idea, first broached in his *Réflexions sur la Révolution de France*, that better ministers would have made the necessary re-forms and prevented a revolution. These reforms would have included the abolition of *lettres de cachet*, the recognition of the right of the Estates-General to approve taxation, the establishment of a system of taxation based on ability to pay and of equality before the law, and the responsibility of all ministers and bureaucrats.[52]

Then, while critical of the administration of the Old Regime, Bertrand de Moleville sought to limit the blame attached to Louis XVI. He had no choice, according to Bertrand, but to assemble the Estates-General because there was a universal call for it, and because the parlements refused to sanction taxation without it. He even sought to excuse Louis XVI from naming the ministers he did, arguing that the King and the Queen did not have much choice but to name Necker in 1788 because he was so popular, and even less choice about calling him back in July of 1789. So the culprit was public opinion, not the King.[53]

He even sought to extricate Louis XVI from responsibility for doubling the Third Estate. The situation, as Bertrand de Moleville observed it, was that the people were ready to revolt. They knew their own strength, and they had no fear of the government. If the King had chosen to dismiss Necker, whom the people adored, rather than to double the Third, it was more than likely that they would have revolted, forced the King to recall Necker, and forced him to double the Third.

He also maintained that it would have been difficult for the King to avoid the specious reasoning that Necker used in arguing for double representation. Bertrand de Moleville said that Necker claimed that the first two estates were against the King; therefore he had to double the Third to rally enough support. Furthermore there were no fixed traditions about the number of deputies for each order. So if he doubled the Third, the King's views would prevail.

The basic problem was that the King could not depend on the loyalty of the army. Bertrand de Moleville claimed that M. de Bouillé had informed the King that of the 200 battalions he commanded he could only count on 5. Furthermore even those troops who were faithful were terrified of the idea of being attacked by a mob armed with sticks and pikes. As far as the nobility were concerned, many had gone over to the Revolution, and the rest did not have enough strength to defend the King.[54]

Then he went back to the character of Louis XVI. The King would never endanger the lives of his soldiers unless he was fairly sure of success. And he would never jeopardize his humblest subject to save himself. Bertrand de Moleville said that Malesherbes once told him: "this extreme sensibility [of Louis XVI], this tenderness of disposition, so amiable in private life . . . often became, in times of revolution, more fatal to a king, than even certain vices would have been."[55] So the mistakes of Louis XVI derived from his virtues. Louis XVI had his weaknesses. He could be indecisive, timid, lacking in energy and self-confidence, and unable to establish his ascendancy over a crowd, but these faults were more the responsibility of his first minister from 1774 to 1781, Maurepas, than of the King himself.[56]

The problem was that Maurepas' successors, if not worse, were at least as bad. Maurepas began the process that led to the Revolution, then the inability and the violence of Loménie de Brienne took the monarchy to the edge of the precipice, and finally the pride and ambition of Necker pushed it over the edge.[57]

Bertrand de Moleville thought that Louis XVI's greatest mistake was to dismiss Calonne before he had ended the meetings of the Assembly of Notables. That step, plus the appointment of Loménie de Brienne, were the immediate causes of the French Revolution. In turning against Calonne, Marie Antoinette let herself be misled by Brienne and by Breteuil. Calonne's only mistake was to be politically naive. He underestimated those seeking to take his place, and he overestimated his ability to persuade his opponents in the Assembly of Notables.[58]

That opened the way to Loménie de Brienne, of whom Bertrand de Moleville was exceedingly critical. After emptying the treasury and destroying public credit, he undermined the power of the monarchy by his excessive use of extraordinary measures, such as lit de justice, lettres de cachets, and banishments and imprisonments, which should only have been employed as a last resort. Bertrand, a former parlementaire, especially objected to his attempt to bypass the parlements in favor of a new Plenary Court.[59]

Brienne's use of excessive measures was shown most clearly and with most consequence in his excessive deployment of the army as a means to overawe his foes. What happened was that the means used to produce fear eventually led to familiarity and contempt. People compared the force exhibited with their own numbers and took courage. Fifty dragoons, prudently managed, might have done better than a host of regiments.[60]

Then the Archbishop of Sens convinced the King to agree to a meeting of the Estates-General in 1789. To make matters worse he encouraged people to publish their ideas on how it should be made up and what it should consider, as if it had never met before and as if they were being invited to set up an entirely new type of government. Loménie de Brienne raised political expectations, and the Revolution fulfilled them.

Next came Necker, who should have realized that a meeting of the Estates-General in such a time of ferment would have disastrous consequences. If he had been as able as claimed he should have solved the fiscal crisis without calling on the Estates-General for help. Furthermore he had so much popular support that he could have delayed a meeting as long as he wished. But he was more interested in power than in the well-being of the state. He thought he could become first minister forever if he had a chance to show off before the Estates-General. So he ushered in a revolution, which was soon to claim him as a victim.[61]

Then Necker was foolish enough to introduce the subject of the doubling of the representation of the Third Estate to the Assembly of Notables and later, against the almost unanimous advice of the Notables, to get Louis XVI to agree to it. He mistakenly thought that, by turning Louis XVI over to the Third Estate, he had rescued him from the clergy and the nobility.[62]

Bertrand then came up with this final assessment of Necker: "Posterity . . . will see in him a man, selfish, ambitious, and vain; foolishly intoxicated with the merit which he believed himself to possess, and jealous of that of others; desirous of excess of honour and of power; virtuous in words and through ostentation more than in reality. In a word, he was a presumptuous empiric in politics and morals; but he was conscientiously so, for he was always the first dupe of his own empiricism."[63]

During the first part of the Directory royalist explanations of the causes of the Revolution mostly covered familiar ground. Montjoie does emphasize the factional divisions of France on the eve of the French Revolution, but one wonders then why those divisions did not facilitate royal conquest. And he does talk about overpopulation, one of the infrequent references of the right wing to the social question. But then he presents such common factors as the philosophes, the physiocrats, and the Calvinists. He also talks about the deficit, the effects of the American Revolution, the borrowing, and the ministers. His main contribution was to emphasize the power of public opinion and the government's inability to cope with it.

Bertrand's explanation of the coming of the Revolution has the merit of not attributing it to some conspiracy from outside. In his account the monarchy fell from within, as a result of its own shortcomings. While recognizing the influence of outside forces, such as the American Revolution, the opposition of the parlements, the resistance of the notables, and the influence of the philosophes, he concentrated on a weak administration that could not institute reform and that embarked on one political folly after another. The King was weak, but Bertrand went out of his way to excuse him and to blame the ministers. Bertrand seems biased in favor of Calonne and against Loménie de Brienne. He also engaged in a good deal of wishful thinking and exaggerated what Necker could have accomplished. Bertrand had the ingredients, but he did not seem to get the proportions right.

During Thermidor and the early years of the Directory, royalist historiography seems to be a in a state of transition. The conspiracy theory was still present. The fault lay with the philosophes, the Calvinists, the ministers, the notables, and with the court of Louis XVI. But at the same time other factors began to come into play. Louis XVI became more responsible than before, there was more emphasis on the need for foreign help, a need keenly felt in contemporary politics, and there was greater recognition of the role played by social factors and by the force of public opinion. So the conspiracy theory, which royalists had found so convenient and so satisfying, was beginning to wan, and royalist accounts were becoming more responsible and more sophisticated.

Starting with Montjoie in his 1797 *Histoire de la révolution de France*, royalists during the Directory also took up basic political and constitutional issues. Montjoie began by asserting that in 1789 Louis XVI was sovereign because all acts emanated from his throne. And he possessed this authority legitimately as his hereditary property. Behind his claims lay providence, which wanted to protect people by organizing them into societies, with a sovereign over each one, and divine and human laws, which protected all property rights. These claims were made explicit in the coronation ceremony which, among other things, elevated the king to the priesthood and made both his person and his authority sacred. The ceremony also called for the obedience of all Catholic Frenchmen. And every person who occupied a position of importance in the country swore an oath of loyalty to the king. So to believe that sovereignty did not belong to the king one would have to deny the rights of property, believe in the disorganization of society, renounce the Catholic religion, and deny the oaths one had sworn.[64]

Montjoie also presented the sovereign as a great father figure.[65] He insisted that in 1789 France had a constitution, and he tried to use a definition of Rousseau to demonstrate the existence of the constitution.[66] Rousseau said that without a constitution there could be a collection of men, but not an association, a people, a state. Since in 1789 France had a people, a state, and a political body, therefore it had a constitution.[67]

He also emphasized that he believed the king was under the law. The king could not and should not want to do anything except what was authorized by the constitution of the state. This meant that groups and individuals were guaranteed all the rights that legitimately belonged to them. The will of the king should be obeyed when it strengthened the constitution and the social pact. Hence the formality of registration—to make sure decrees followed the constitution and did not injure either the general interest or that of individuals.[68]

Montjoie then attacked Montesquieu, whom he said was popular because of his ability to invent catchy phrases. By this means Montesquieu was able to put over his idea that the legislature should be divided into two houses. And the encyclopedists believed in his principles and were responsible for spreading them. Also Montesquieu's writings inspired imitators. The worst effect was that they turned people toward the study of politics, which led to a political mania, which in turn had so many disastrous consequences![69]

Bertrand de Moleville also contributed to the constitutional debate. His first work during this period, an abstract of much that would follow, was a pamphlet entitled *Réflexions sur la Révolution de France*. He also maintained that France under the Old Regime did indeed have a constitution, even though its laws were not passed by a legislature (as in England). Bertrand de Moleville maintained that France had its own charters and statutes, such as the Salic Law. He said that the king as sovereign issued the laws, and he sought to use Blackstone and Montesquieu to buttress his position.[70]

Bertrand de Moleville argued that in all governments, whether monarchical, aristocratic, or democratic, sovereignty was the same. In all of them it was "absolute, irresistible," and it had "the right to make new laws and to repeal old ones." If such power were despotic, then all governments were despotic. The only difference was that in democracies it was the despotism of a multitude, in aristocracies the despotism of a few, and in monarchies the despotism of one. There had to be a supreme authority, or governments would not be able to exist. The problem, he thought, was that too many people confused absolute power, which was a necessary element of all governments, with arbitrary power, which was a degradation of it.[71]

On the same point he went on to assert that the welfare of states always depended on a wise combination of legislative and executive authority. The idea that they had to be separated was absurd and disastrous. It was as ridiculous as the idea that France was despotic because it had prisons, as if other states did not, and because it was possible for some ministers to abuse the *lettres de cachet*, as if the executive branch was not subject to abuse in all states. Since the lettres de cachet were not authorized by any law, it would be a simple thing to abolish them forever. What had actually happened, he believed, was that the fear of despotism had led France during the Revolution to adopt a form of government that was a thousand times more despotic than anything else in its history.[72]

Warming to the theme of despotism, de Moleville claimed that despotism was not a true form of government, but rather an abuse to which all governments were subject. Furthermore it was perhaps less likely to occur when power was in the hands of one person than when it was held by several. The best constitution, he thought, was the one that raised the most barriers to despotism, and perhaps the constitution of the Old Regime in France offered the most advantages in this regard. Surely the French Republic with its revolutionary tribunals, its requisitions, and its law of the maximum had demonstrated that under the reign of several, despotism was much more violent than under the reign of one.[73]

It was possible, he admitted, for a very weak king to have a despotic first minister. Cardinal Richelieu provided such an example. But it was much more likely for weak kings to have weak ministers, as incapable as the kings were in guiding the ship of state. How this was an effective argument for monarchy is unclear! In any case Bertrand de Moleville said that this was the greatest fault of monarchies. For example he asserted that if a strong minister like Maupeou had remained in place, instead of being succeeded by weak ministers like Maurepas and Necker, the French Revolution probably would not have occurred.[74]

Returning to his thesis that the French monarchy was not despotic, he pointed his finger at the intermediary bodies, which Montesquieu had cited as protection against despotism. Bertrand de Moleville identified them as the Estates-General, the provincial estates, and the parlements, the latter in charge of registering, promulgating, and maintaining the laws that formed the constitution. Only laws established by the parlements had to be followed, and the laws bound both the monarchy and his subjects, whereas the despot could do whatever he wished.[75]

Bertrand de Moleville then went back to the question of how to avoid irresponsible or weak ministers. It was easy to establish, he thought, that the French Revolution broke out at a time when the ministers were incapable. But this was not the result of the traditional French constitution, under which the King, until the end of the fifteenth century, selected the first President of the parlements and the Chancellor from lists of nominees submitted by the judges. It would be easy, he believed, to return to such a system, to extend it, and to refine it so that only the most highly qualified were eligible for appointment to the top offices.[76]

Bertrand de Moleville began his *Private Memoirs* with an argument that monarchy was preferable to a republic on the following grounds:

> 1st. That the more extensive and populous an empire is, the more power is required to be placed in the hand of Government:
>
> 2d. The power of Government diminishes in proportion to the number of hands which exercise it. The more people there are in any country to command, the fewer will there be to obey:
>
> 3d. That popular elections are more favorable to intriguing, restless, and wrong-headed men, than to prudent and virtuous citizens:
>
> 4th. That the expense of Administration is infinitely more considerable in a republic than in a monarchy; because in the first, a greater number must have employments.[77]

In the last part of his memoirs Bertrand de Moleville abandoned his running commentary on the course of events and returned to the discussion of constitutional issues, which he had first broached in his *Réflexions* of 1796. He asserted again that one did not have to have a written constitution to have a constitutional government. He pointed to England as an example where the entire body of legislation made up the constitution; the same thing was true of France. Laws were permanent and binding, whether they were collected in a great charter or not.[78]

He also reiterated the notion that political absolutism was not despotic, quoting Blackstone to help make his case. The problem, he maintained was that people confused absolute with arbitrary government. "The sovereign power must always be absolute in every government whatever.[79] The moment it ceases to be such, and finds a resistance which it cannot overcome, the resisting force becomes, in fact, the supreme power, insurrection annihilates legal authority, and the government no longer exists."[80] It was only arbitrary power that was despotic.

He also took up the assertion, first raised in his *Réflexions* but now discussed at greater length, that monarchy was the best defense against despotism. Despotism stemmed from people who wanted power and riches. Princes, who already had them, were not motivated by them. These passions were found, instead, in the masses and in those who hoped to profit from mass unrest.

Moreover the French system possessed the intermediate and subordinate powers that Montesquieu had talked about as necessary checks on authority. In fact the French problem was that the intermediate powers were too strong and they were not subordinate enough. If the nobility "had taken less advantage of the state of weakness to which they themselves had reduced the government, even the fatal deficit might have been passed over without violent effect. We should then have had neither assemblies of notables, nor states general, nor a republic: we should now be in possession of all we have lost."[81] Such was Bertrand de Moleville's understanding of the effects of the aristocratic resurgence. So if the French monarchy was restored one should be less concerned to strengthen the intermediate powers than to regulate and to limit them.[82]

Bertrand then borrowed from his experience in England to suggest that the ministry and the bureaucracy in France would improve if, as in England, the French had a prime minister who would nominate the other members of the council. What had happened under the Old Regime was that intrigue and favor had determined place. In fact the French Revolution took place at a time when almost all of the chief positions were filled by incapable people. If a system of appointment on the basis of merit were established, on the other hand, "the administration would always be composed of the ablest men of the nation, and all public employments would be filled by men of talent and integrity."[83]

He then combatted the notion that the French could be governed by an assembly. "The French," he said, "have too much vivacity and petulance to be capable of carrying on a cold methodical discussion upon any subject whatever. Ten or twelve, even of the wisest and most judicious, cannot continue a conversation, on any interesting subject, for a quarter of an hour, without a degree of heat, which assumes the appearance, and sometimes the nature, of a quarrel; all of them speaking at once, and all being more capable, and more inclined, to speak than to listen. . . ."[84] It was worse in a national assembly: there tumult would be the order of the day. One could not expect effective legislation from such a body, which would act emotionally and precipitously. The only means to handle such an assembly would be by influence and corruption, but the expense of the latter would impose a groaning load of taxation on the nation.

For France, then, the best prescription was a monarch, assisted by effective ministers. "France would then be truly regenerated. . . . and all the seeds of sedition and revolution would be blasted for ever."[85] Since this was the case, what the European powers should do, as he explained in his *Annals*, was to establish a coalition, recognize Louis XVIII as King, and proceed to free the French from their revolutionary oppressors. The King should move to the frontier of the country and call up his subjects to join him, both those who had remained loyal and those who repented of their political follies. Then the era of Jacobinism would be over at last.[86]

At a time when the monarchy had its best chance since 1789, apologists for the monarchy thus laid down principles and proposed reforms. They argued that France in 1789 had a living constitution with traditions, precedents, restraints, and laws. It had the kind of intermediary bodies that Montesquieu talked about, though some of them, like the parlements, in fact became too strong. Despotism then came only with the French Revolution. The constitution of the Directory, on the other hand, borrowed principles from Montesquieu and from the British constitution that were completely unworkable.

And these apologists for monarchy were willing to make concessions and reforms. They now advocated abolishing the lettres de cachet and establishing taxation based on ability to pay, equality before the law, and responsible ministers and bureaucrats. They even gave suggestions about how to select good ministers. Finally at least one of them was ready to recognize the right of the Estates-General to approve taxation. So some of them had gone a long way toward recognizing the abuses of the Old Regime and towards formulating a program that might bring them support in the future.

NOTES

A version of this chapter was given at the Consortium on Revolutionary Europe at Charleston, South Carolina in February of 1989 and printed in the *Proceedings of the Consortium on Revolutionary Europe*, 18 (1990), II, 95–110.

1. *Nouvelle Biographie Générale*, 17 (1856), col. 493; Antoine François Claude, comte de Ferrand, *Mémoires du comte Ferrand, Ministre d'état sous Louis XVIII* (Paris, 1897), viii–ix.

2. Antoine François Claude, comte de Ferrand, *Des Causes qui ont empêche la contre-révolution en France, et Considérations sur la révolution sociale; suivies d'une notice sur Robespierre et ses complices* (Berne, 1795), 5.

3. Ibid., 6.
4. Ibid., 7–8.
5. Ibid., 15, 17.
6. Ibid., 40–43, 46–48.
7. Ibid., 65.

8. Claude Bellanger, Jacques Godechot, Pierre Guiral, and Fernand Terrou, eds., *Histoire général de la presse française*, I (Paris, 1969), 526.

9. *La Quotidienne*, August 27, 1795.

10. Jeremy D. Popkin, *The Right-Wing Press in France, 1792–1800* (Chapel Hill, 1980), 145–46.

11. Jean Thomas Langlois, *Des Gouvernements qui ne conviennent pas à la France* (Paris, 1795), 3.

12. *Ferrand, Des Causes qui ont empêche la contre-révolution en France*, 162ff.

13. Ibid., 222.

14. Ibid., 222–23.

15. Ibid., 224–25.

16. Ibid., 226–27.

17. Ibid., 228–29.

18. Gabriel Sénac de Meilhan, *Du gouvernement, des moeurs, et des conditions en France, avant la révolution; avec le caractère des principaux personnages du règne de Louis XVI* (Hamburg, 1795), 14.

19. Ibid., 15.

20. Ibid., 83–84.

21. Ibid., 126.

22. Jean Thomas Langlois, *Des Gouvernemens qui ne conviennent pas à la France* (Paris, 1795), 11–12.

23. Ibid., 24. Jean Thomas Richer-Sérizy took the same line against the separation of powers in the royalist newspaper *Accusateur publique*, nos. 9–11 (1795), 56, as cited in Popkin, *The Right-Wing Press in France*, 207 n. 83.

24. Ibid., 35–39.

25. Ibid., 40, 52.

26. Ibid., 61, 68–69.

27. Ibid., 75–76.

28. Jean Thomas Langlois, *Qu'est-ce qu'une Convention nationale?* (Paris, 1795), 25.

29. Ibid., 29.

30. Ibid., 43.

31. Jean Thomas Langlois, *De la Souveraineté* (Paris, 1797), 1, 37, 49.

32. Christophe Félix Louis Ventre de la Touloubre Montjoie, *Éloge historique et funèbre de Louis XVIe du nom, roi de France et de Navarre* (Neuchâtel, 1796), xvii.

33. Ibid., 73–74, 78. As far as Montjoie was concerned, the wars of the French Revolution would dispose of the dregs of the surplus population, and France would then return to its rightful government, the legitimate descendants of Louis XVI. Ibid., 77–78.

34. Ibid., 79–80.

35. Ibid., 82–83.

36. Ibid., 93–96.

37. Ibid., 96–97.

38. Ibid., 104–5. Actually according to Leo Gershoy, though Turgot reduced government expenses, Louis XVI did not cut down on pensions, gifts, and court expenses. *The French Revolution and Napoleon* (New York, 1933), 91.

39. Ibid., 107–8.

40. Ibid., 81–82, 116–17.

41. Here he referred to the machinations of John Law.

42. *Christophe Félix Louis Ventre de la Touloubre Montjoie, Histoire de la révolution de France, Depuis la présentation au parlement de l'impôt territorial et de celui du timbre, jusqu'à la conversion des états généraux en assemblée nationale (Paris, 1797)*, I, 225.

43. Ibid., I, 225–26, 228, 230–31.

44. Ibid., I, 264.

45. Ibid., I, 245–46.

46. *Dictionnaire de biographie française*, 6 (Paris, 1954), cols. 288–90; *Nouvelle Biographie Générale*, 5 (Paris, 1860), cols. 772–73; Elphège Boursin and Augustin Challamel, eds., *Dictionnaire de la Révolution française* (Paris, 1893), 174; Antoine François Bertrand de Moleville, *Private Memoirs Relative to the Last Year of the Reign of Lewis the Sixteenth, Late King of France* (Paris, 1797), I, 54–55, 121, 126; II, 153–56; E. Bertrand, "Un ministre de la marine sous Louis XVI: Bertrand de Molleville, *Revue des études historiques*, 97 (1931), 411–30; H. A. Barton, "The Origins of the Brunswick Manifesto," *French Historical Studies* IV (Fall, 1967), 153–54; Beik, *The French Revolution Seen from the Right*, 99.

47. Antoine François Bertrand de Moleville, *Private Memoirs Relative to the Last Year of the Reign of Lewis the Sixteenth, Late King of France* (London, 1797), 3 vols.; *Mémoires secrets pour servir à l'histoire de la dernière année du régne de Louis XVI* (London, 1797), 3 vols.; *Mémoires particuliers pour servir à l'histoire de la fin du règne de Louis XVI* (Paris, 1816), 2 vols.

48. *Annals of the French Revolution; or a Chronological account of its principal events; with a variety of anecdotes and characters hitherto unpublished . . .* (London, 1800), 4 vols.; 2d Ed. (London, 1809), vols. 5–9. A French version was called *Histoire de la Révolution pendant les dernières années du règne de Louis XVI* (Paris, 1801–1802), 10 vols.

49. Antoine François Bertrand de Moleville, *Annals of the French Revolution*, I, x.

50. Ibid., Chapter I, unpaged.

51. Ibid.

52. Bertrand de Moleville, *Private Memoirs*, I, 20–22.

53. Ibid., I, 23–24.

54. Ibid., I, 27–28. Bouillé's assertions that only 5 of the 200 military battalions would support the King is confirmed by J. M. Thompson, *The French Revolution* (Oxford, 1951), 44.

55. Ibid., 29.

56. Ibid., I, 28–30.

57. Ibid., I, 36.

58. Ibid., I, 42–44.

59. Ibid., I, 46–47.

60. Ibid., I, 57–58.

61. Ibid., I, 116–19.

62. Ibid., I, 158–59.

63. Ibid., I, 177–78.

64. Montjoie, *Histoire de la révolution de France*, I, 31–32.

65. Ibid., I, 54.

66. Ibid., I, 139.

67. Ibid., I, 141. Rousseau actually said: "There will always be a great difference between subduing a multitude and governing a society. When organized men are successfully subjugated by one individual, whatever number they may be of them, they appear to me only as a master and slaves; I cannot regard them as a people and their chief; but they are, if you please, an *aggregation*, but they are not as yet an *association*; for there is neither public property, nor a political body, among them." *The Social Contract*. Edited by Charles Frankel (New York, 1947), Book I, chapter 5, 13.

68. Ibid., I, 155.

69. Ibid., I, 33.

70. Antoine François Bertrand de Moleville, *Réflexions sur la Révolution de France, et sur les erreurs le plus généralement adoptées relativement á l'ancienne constitution de ce royaume, et au prétendu despotisme de son gouvernement* (London, 1796), 6–17.

71. Ibid., 18–19.

72. Ibid., 27–28.

73. Ibid., 28–29, 33.

74. Ibid., 32.

75. Ibid., 37–38.

76. Ibid., 47–48.

77. Bertrand de Moleville, *Private Memoires Relative to the Last Year of the Reign of Lewis the Sixteenth*, I, 14–15.

78. *Private Memoirs*, III, 330–31.

79. Whether it be democratic, aristocratic, or monarchical government.

80. Ibid., III, 334–37.

81. Ibid., III, 363–64.

82. *Private Memoirs*, III, 348–49, 363–64; see also *Mémoires particuliers*, II, 415–16.

83. Ibid., III, 366–68.

84. Ibid., III, 371–72.

85. Ibid., III, 375–76.

86. *Annals of the French Revolution*, I, xli–xlii.

CHAPTER VI

Du Voisin, Bossuet, and the French Revolution

The abbé Jean Baptiste Du Voisin (1744–1813), former canon of Laon, was the author of the 1789 *La France chrétienne, juste et vraiment libre*, and who published *Examen des principes de la Révolution françoise* in exile in 1795, with expanded versions of this work under the title *Défense de l'ordre social, contre les principes de la Révolution française* published in 1798 and 1801. He began the *Examen* with a very gloomy assessment of the effects of the Revolution. Wherever its principles prevailed, "laws will remain without force, passions without check, property without guarantee. Everywhere they penetrate, they will carry with them anarchy, brigandage and immorality."[1]

After asserting that society could not survive without government and that there could be no government without sovereign power located somewhere in it, he undertook a survey of the forms of government. Despotism existed when one person governed without any restrictions on his will; monarchy when the ruler followed "fixed and established laws"; a republic when sovereignty rested in the people as a group, as was the case in a democracy, or in some of the people, as in an aristocracy.[2]

Furthermore he explained what he meant by moderate governments. They were the ones that recognized a constitution, "the fundamental laws that fix and limit the exercise of the sovereign power." Constitutional government existed in every state where no one could be deprived of life, liberty, or property except by lawful means, and where one could lawfully appeal any arbitrary decision.[3]

And he made a special point of distinguishing absolute governments from despotic ones. Despotism was identified by its arbitrary nature. Absolute power was not arbitrary if there were fundamental laws that the ruler could not modify. Every government had to be absolute; authority had to be able to overcome resistance. It did not matter whether authority was vested in the people, or in a senate, or in a monarch, or whether each of them had a part of it. Without sovereignty there would be anarchy. But it had to be subject to laws and to constitutional procedure; otherwise there would be despotism.[4]

Du Voisin attributed the French Revolution to a conspiracy in which the philosophes played a major role. Although they had the ambition to win the reputation of the great writers of the seventeenth century, they lacked the talent. So they made a name for themselves by their bold and singular paradoxes. They astonished the unknowing, who thought their old errors were new discoveries. They attracted the most vicious people, and they won over the youth, who took their religion from Voltaire, their ethics from Helvetius, and their public law from Raynal. First the philosophes only asked for tolerance and for freedom of thought. But their arrogance, their fanatical zeal, and their efforts to control public opinion made it clear that they wanted to destroy the Christian religion. According to Du Voisin, Rousseau predicted that if the philosophes ever attained power they would be more intolerant than anyone else. When they became all powerful under the Revolution, the prediction was found to be true.[5]

The philosophes were joined by Freemasons, by courtisans, and by others, who for a long time had been conspiring to overthrow religion and monarchy. The incapacity of Loménie de Brienne, the errors of the parlements, the mistaken calling of the Estates-General, and the treachery of Necker provided the opportunity. The conspirators stirred up the people in the name of liberty. They also raised the illusion of equality to a people who, though enjoying abundance and peace, thought they were humbled by the superior orders. Du Voisin said they did not realize a general leveling would press the people down more than it raised them up.[6]

Du Voisin then turned to a defense of monarchy and began with the argument that monarchy was the best form of government for a large state. Monarchy was most effective and efficient. A republic would not work because France was too large and made up of too many different peoples. Furthermore, following Montesquieu, for a republic there had to be a large amount of public spiritedness. The French, however, while the most civilized people in Europe, were at the same time the most corrupt. France was plunged into vice, into luxury, into license, and above all into philosophical egoism, which destroyed all social feelings. These were the causes of the French Revolution. France was too vicious to support monarchy, which was the government that asked least of its people. How could it ever be kept in check by a democratic government, which demanded the most![7]

Du Voisin then returned to the subject of sovereignty and argued that it was created in an absolute and irrevocable fashion. Though the people did not want to give a ruler the power to rule arbitrarily, they thought it better to be subject to temporary abuses than to leave room for factions and disorder. If there was to be peace and tranquility the sovereign should not be subject to any judicial authority. In establishing laws and sovereign power the people gave up the right to create their own justice. Every insurrection, no matter what the cause, was an infraction of the social pact.[8]

Du Voisin expanded on the same theme in his *Défense de l'ordre social.* Here he said that even in a case of definite oppression it was wrong for individuals to engage in active resistance. Such resistance would lead inevitably to the destruction of society. Society could no longer exist if each citizen had the right to engage in insurrection. Even under the most liberal constitutions, with the most enlightened government, it was likely that there would be some injustice because princes and magistrates were only human. Such injustice was nothing compared to the troubles and disorders of a state of anarchy. So it would be foolish to try to destroy society and return to a state of nature, where everybody would be fighting against everybody else. The welfare of all was the most important thing. Particular interests should bow before the general interest. "An injustice committed by a sovereign is particular and passing, but resistance to authority . . . is a general and permanent wrong because it attacks public order, on which depends the safety of all."[9]

Then he described the horrible effects of popular revolution. Those who participated in mass uprisings were not interested in disputing who should be in charge, but in destroying authority. They wanted to be free and did not think they were until they had trampled on all the laws. They saw the best institutions as only abuses. Skillful at destruction, they were unable to effect any reforms. Whereas rebellions were temporary sicknesses that often revived the state and gave it new strength, popular revolutions led to complete disorganization and to the dissolution of the political body.[10]

In *Examen des principes* Du Voisin said there were definite sanctions against revolts. Sovereigns and peoples were linked by mutual obligations that went back to the contract that established the political association in the first place. This contract did not expire when the ruler failed to live up to its conditions because of two factors. The first was that people could not be happy unless they had peace. And they almost always suffered more from the effects of revolution than they did from temporary abuses of the existing government.[11]

The second restraint was a legalistic one. In a case where one of the contracting parties was not living up to its obligations, the terms of the annulment of the contract should be spelled out either by the contract itself or by an impartial judge, and not by the party that had a grievance. Otherwise it would be possible to evade commitments on the most frivolous of charges. In the case of governments whose power was not limited by a constitution, the government itself was the only judge when there were complaints. And if the original agreement did not tell how the contract could be broken, such determination could be made by no human power because the sovereign and the subjects recognized no common judge. In such cases, as in marriage, the social contract was unbreakable. The unfaithfulness of one of the parties did not give the other party its freedom.[12]

In *Défense de l'ordre social* Du Voisin argued that it was because the sovereign was for the people that it had to be separate from them. He maintained an authority that could be judged by the people would not have enough strength to protect them from their own weaknesses.[13]

In fact, as Bossuet made clear, following the original social pact the sovereign was not answerable to any member of his administration, nor liable to any punishment from anyone. He was subject to no tribunal, no judge, and no sentence. To have a well-ordered state one had to bestow upon the sovereign a kind of infallibility. Everything became mixed up and unclear if one tried to make the sovereign accountable, even more so if the sovereign was subject to the judgments, which meant the whims, of the crowd. Du Voisin claimed that the people should prefer bad government to the disorder that would arise from resisting a sovereign power.[14]

After a long quotation from Bossuet's *Politique Sacrée*, Du Voisin concluded this section on sovereign power with the pious hope that people of all classes would forget about political factionalism and about innovation, and let the passage of time gradually bring the necessary reforms. He also hoped they would come to realize that it was in their interest to uphold the established government.[15]

Then, tackling the subject of absolute monarchy and liberty in *Examen des principes*, he said that Rousseau was wrong to claim that absolute power was contrary to natural right and that if people submitted to it they would inevitably fall into slavery. Absolute power, in cases where it was guaranteed by a constitution, actually maintained civil liberty. That was the difference between absolute monarchy and despotism. Following Bossuet, Du Voisin asserted that people who submitted to a king did not lose their liberty, but received an inviolable safeguard for it. They voluntarily sacrificed some of their natural rights so they could enjoy the rest of them in peace and safety.[16]

Du Voisin emphasized the limits on absolute power. Since the sovereign was not a despot, the subjects were not slaves. Although not subject to the penalties of the law, the ruler was under the law. And in all moderate governments, including absolute monarchy, there were fundamental laws that the prince could never break. Whatever attacked these sacred laws was null and void. One did not have to obey these violations, and, in fact, one should resist them, as long as one did not endanger the state.[17]

For France these fundamental laws included the hereditary succession to the throne, the privileges of the three orders, the rights of the provinces, the right to agree to new taxes, the registering and publishing of laws by the parlements, and the right of each citizen to be judged by a court of law. These fundamental laws were the expression of the general law at the time the state was born.[18]

If a prince did violate the fundamental laws, Du Voisin emphasized, as Bossuet did, that subjects could not mount armed resistance. They could not make war against the sovereign, who had a monopoly on armed force. Resistance then should be negative; while refusing to obey unconstitutional commands, one should maintain an attitude of submission in all things that were not against the constitution. And in doubtful cases the authority of the state should prevail. One should obey only the ruler, who was the father of all. As a son could never offer armed resistance to the unjust wishes of his father, after trying prayers, remonstrances, and protests, the subject could only wait patiently for the righting of wrongs, either by the prince or by his successor.[19]

It was just by this combination of tenacity and moderation that the parlements were able to stop the initiatives of certain kings when they were too arbitrary. Without endangering the State, they were able to preserve the French constitution, if not entirely, at least without any changes but those that came inevitably with the evolution of time, the change of customs, and the inconstancy of human nature.[20]

It was not true that the idea of submitting to authority served only to increase the power of bad rulers. Kings realized that men were often motivated by interests rather than by principles. They realized that people pushed to the limit were not stopped by moral principles, and that they thought only of their own grievances. As Bossuet indicated, power pushed too far ended up destroying itself; oppression led to rebellion; the mistakes of kings were punished by the crimes of the people. If the idea of submission to authority kept the people in check under good kings, in spite of unavoidable abuses, it was not strong enough to restrain them against bad rulers. The people needed to depend on the government for their well being; the government needed to have the people find their happiness in the exercise of its authority.[21]

Du Voisin repeated many of these points on the limits of absolute power in his *Défense de l'ordre sociale*.[22] He emphasized that every citizen had the right to civil liberty, by which he meant the right to submit only to the law. There could be no other legitimate authority but the law. Every arbitrary exercise of power was illegal. And the sovereign himself was subject to the law; if he violated it he would accomplish nothing. There were, however, some exceptional cases where the public welfare called for the ruler to put himself above the law. Such action was excused by the general law that gave the sovereign whatever power was necessary for the safety of the state.[23]

He also explained that one thing setting monarchy apart from despotism was that in despotism the officers of the government were directly under the control of the ruler. In a monarchy, on the other hand, although the ruler was the source of all power, he could not exercise it by himself, nor arbitrarily withdraw it from others. As a result, there was more political equality under a despot, but very little civil equality.[24]

He also argued that the maxim, "whatever the king wishes, the law wishes,"[25] did not apply to the fundamental laws of the state, but only to the secondary and administrative laws that came from the king. The king ruled only by law and did not have the authority to do whatever he wanted. "In conferring upon him legislative power for everything that was related to the government, the constitution subjects him to the laws that he did not make, which are the expression of the general will, either at the birth of the monarchy, or at more recent periods, which cannot be abrogated except on the request and with the express approval of the nation convened and assembled according to the ancient and legitimate forms."[26] So Du Voisin was willing to make use of Rousseau's concept of the general will to limit the power of the monarchy.

The excuse of past uprisings had been that the people were being oppressed. As he had made clear, such uprisings were never legitimate. But the excuse was particularly inappropriate in the revolt against Louis XVI. Every year of his reign had seen benefits and reforms. His mistakes stemmed from the wishes of the people, whom he was completely devoted to. His worst fault was to defer in his selection of ministers to the will of the people, which was often only the voice of a cabal.[27]

Du Voisin then mounted a stiff defense of social and political hierarchy. He said that if one wanted to go back to the origins of political hierarchy, one could find it in the difference in strength and talent of the property holders. But whatever the origins, once established by law or confirmed by the passage of time, the distinctions between the classes and the privileges that resulted from them were sacred property rights that were bound up with public order. They could not be attacked without undermining the foundations of the constitution.

He argued that in a well-ordered state, the prerogatives of the upper classes served to defend and guarantee the rights of the lower classes. A blow against the top ranks threatened all the people. Once the sacred principle of property was encroached upon, one would not be able to say where the plunder would stop. The law that suppressed the hereditary nobility in France alerted the bourgeoisie that the forced requisition of money, goods, and soldiers would come next. "Thus in our ancient constitution the different orders of the State, each animated by a particular spirit, contributed to the general welfare. Thus the privileges of the first two orders and the political rights that the Parlements possessed formed a barrier against despotism, and civil equality was affirmed by political inequality."[28]

Du Voisin then attacked the idea of popular sovereignty. Though he conceded that sovereignty derived originally from the people's consent, he insisted that the people did not possess it, nor had they ever done so. Sovereignty did not begin until some government was invested with it. "Before the social pact that gave birth to sovereignty the people were not sovereign; they were only independent. As a result of the social pact they ceased to be independent and became subjects."[29]

Next Du Voisin took on Rousseau's notion of popular sovereignty. The only examples of its operation in history, he said, were turbulent ones because the people were unfit to govern. Not only were they unable to exercise the functions of the government or of the executive power, which he said even Rousseau himself admitted, but also they could not handle any political administration and hence any exercise of sovereignty.[30]

The very idea that the people could legislate was ridiculous. They were impetuous, ignorant, and changeable. There never had been legislation by a large assembly. The best laws were those issued by absolute sovereigns because they were above any personal interest. Even if the ruler was lacking in virtue, reason showed him that his interests were inseparable from those of the society as a whole.

So sovereignty did not belong to the people because the people them-selves needed to be governed. They could not manage legislation because the purpose of legislation was to keep them in check. And they could not control armed force because then there would not be any power left to restrain them.[31]

He believed that the French Revolution offered the proof of these assertions. As soon as they boasted that they had obtained freedom, the French people found themselves subdued in turn by the National Assembly, by the clubs, by Robespierre, by the Convention, and then by the Directory. Since they were unable to govern themselves, they had to submit to rulers, who soon turned themselves into dictators.[32]

In *Examen des principes* Du Voisin next took up the relationship between religion and political authority. Continuing to borrow from Bossuet, he maintained that although the people originally decided on the form of government and even selected the person who would assume power, God really conferred authority. All authority came from God, who was the creator and who was all powerful. God, the supreme leader of society and the arbiter of life and death, established the prince to defend the good and to chastise the bad. God made the prince sacred and reserved for Himself the right to judge him. It was in the presence of God "that the Sovereign swears to govern, to protect, and to defend the people, and that the people swear to obey the Sovereign."[33] By this means the ruler and the subjects made an engagement with God that was even closer than the one they made with each other. Thereafter politics and religion remained closely linked. Rebellion and tyranny were not just crimes against the state, but sacrilege. Revolt was an attack on God in the person of his representative; tyranny was the evil use of power that came from the source of all good.

Authority that stemmed only from the wishes of the people would be unreliable: those who gave it would think they had the right to take it away. Though one might argue on behalf of the original contract and cite the need for public order, it would be easy to break human conventions and to find pretexts in the general interest. By such reasoning revolt might be imprudent, but it would not be a crime. The only thing that would reconcile the personal interest with the general interest was the will of God. Sovereign power came from God, and whoever challenged authority challenged an order created by God Himself.[34]

As Bossuet indicated, the purpose of authority was to promote the welfare and the safety of the subjects. A king was not the ruler for his own sake, but for others. His subjects were not his property, but his trust. Even though he could receive no earthly judgment, his conscience and the cries of the oppressed would call him before the tribunal of the Lord. Authority stripped away pride when it stemmed from God, before whom kings were nothing and to whom kings had to make an accounting of their stewardship. People owed the ruler respect, obedience, and faithfulness as part of their religious duties because sovereign power came from divine power. Kings were "the second Majesty after God." But kings owed the people prosperity, peace, and happiness.[35]

Du Voisin pursued the relationship between religion and politics in his *Défense de l'ordre social.* Here he asserted that the social order was annulled when one tried to separate it from religion; only when the connection was restored could it exist. Furthermore, without the presence of the Supreme Being, the social pact had no force. Building on the foundation of Bossuet, he maintained that without God there was no penetration of the conscience and nothing to restrain the passions. Religion held society together. Without it men were isolated, divided, and separated from all the ties that linked them with each other and with the sovereign.[36]

Given the above assumptions it was clear to him that what France should do was to restore the Bourbon monarchy. Only it could free France from civil and foreign wars. Any other choice would be the work of a faction and would signal a new revolution and a new civil war. If the French were so foolish as to reject the candidate offered them by God, then they would continue to struggle to see who would be their tyrant. Then France would move from republican anarchy to the anarchy of an elected despot.[37]

On the causes of the French Revolution, Du Voisin offered what was by then the rather hackneyed right-wing argument that it stemmed from a conspiracy. While recognizing that the Old Regime had made some mistakes, the Revolution was basically the result of the agitation of the philosophes and others. Du Voisin and others on the Right offered a myth of the Old Regime, which made the Revolution unnecessary and inappropriate.[38] In this account the Old Regime became a time of peace and abundance, and the reign of Louis XVI one of ongoing reforms and improvements.

Du Voisin tried to apply old political theories to the problems raised by the Revolution. In the processs he called on such diverse figures as Bossuet, Rousseau, Montesquieu, and possibly Hobbes to help him out. Throughout his analysis he was preoccupied with the need to restore order. Although I find his discussion of sovereignty unpersuasive, he thought that in definitely establishing it he could avoid anarchy. Given his concern he emphasized the horrible effects of popular revolution and offered sanctions, some more convincing than others, against revolution. In this regard he offered a utilitarian argument that kings had to rule well or people would resist, though he offered no evidence that they did rule well. For Du Voisin the class system and the privileges associated with it also served as guarantees of order. His assertion that religion promoted order and restrained the passions reflected the utilitarian approach toward religion in the Enlightenment and anticipated those nineteenth-century liberals and conservatives who said that religion was good for the people because it helped keep them in line.

Du Voisin came out for gradual change, which links him with the organic theory of history and means that he is not a complete reactionary. But in cases where there was no constitution, he stacked the deck in favor of established governments and left aggrieved subjects without recourse. Furthermore, he continued to emphasize order at the expense of accountability. He did emphasize the limits on absolutism, citing especially the fundamental laws. And he recognized the right of the people to resist peacefully if those laws were broken, although he gave them no alternative if peaceful measures did not work.

He launched a spirited attack on popular sovereignty, asserting that although the people had conferred it, somehow they had never possessed it. And if they did get their hands on it, as the French Revolution demonstrated, the result was chaos. So Du Voisin tried to employ precedent, tradition, the precepts of Bossuet, and practical arguments to lead France from the chaos of the Revolution to a restoration of the Bourbon monarchy, which alone could restore peace, liberty, and order.

NOTES

A version of this chapter was presented at the Society for French Historical Studies in March of 1990. It was prepared with the assistance of Prof. Harry R. Davis of Beloit College.

1. [Jean Baptiste Du Voisin] *Examen des principes de la Révolution françoise* (Wolfenbuttel, 1795), 2.

2. Ibid., 6–7.

3. Ibid., 9.

4. Ibid., 10; *Défense de l'ordre social, contre les principes de la Révolution française*, Nouv. ed. (Leipzig, 1801), 19.

5. *Examen des principes*, 97–98. I can find no such reference in Rousseau.

6. Ibid., 4.

7. *Défense de l'ordre social*, 23, 233.

8. *Examen des principes*, 51, 70. Du Voisin does not cite Hobbes, but the emphasis he places on sovereign power may have come from him. At least there are some similarities:

> The only way to erect such a common power, as may be able to defend them from the invasion of foreigners, and the injuries of one another, and thereby to secure them in such sort as that by their own industry and by the fruits of the earth they may nourish themselves and live contentedly, is to confer all their power and strength upon one man, or upon one assembly of men, that may reduce all their wills, by plurality of voices unto one will . . . and therein to submit their wills, every one to his will, and their judgements to his judgement.

Thomas Hobbes, *Leviathan, Or, Matter, Form, and Power of a Commonwealth Ecclesiastical and Civil* (Chicago, 1952), chap. 17, 100.

Another similarity includes:

they that are subjects to a monarch cannot without his leave cast off monarchy and return to the confusion of a disunited multitude; nor transfer their person from him that beareth it to another man, or another assembly of men: for they are bound, every man to every man, to own and be reputed author of all that he that already is their sovereign shall do and judge fit to be done. . . . Secondly, because the right of bearing the person of them all is given to him they make sovereign, by covenant only of one to another, and not of him to any of them, there can happen no breach of covenant on the part of the sovereign; and consequently none of his subjects, by any pretense of forfeiture, can be freed from his subjection

Hobbes, *Leviathan*, chap. 18, 101.

9. *Défense de l'ordre social*, 100. See Jacques Bénigne Bossuet, *Politique tirée des propres paroles de l'Écriture sainte*, Edition critique avec introduction et notes par Jacques Le Brun (Geneva, 1967), 192. Bossuet said that those who resisted should be sentenced to death.

10. *Défense de l'ordre social*, 106.

11. Here again is the possible influence of Hobbes: "the sovereign power . . . is as great as possibly men can be imagined to make it. And though of so unlimited a power, men may fancy many evil consequences, yet the consequence of the want of it, which is perpetual war of every man against his neighbour, are much worse. . . . In those nations whose Commonwealths have been long-lived, and not destroyed by foreign war, the subjects never did dispute of the sovereign power," Hobbes, *Leviathan*, chapter 20, 112.

12. *Examen des principes*, 72–74. The same issue is discussed in *Défense de l'ordre social*, 111–16.

13. *Défense de l'ordre social*, 124.

14. Ibid., 125–26. Bossuet, *Politique tirée des propres paroles de l'Écriture sainte*, 92–93.

15. *Défense de l'ordre social*, 129.

16. *Examen des principes*, 75–76; almost exactly the same text is given in *Défense de l'ordre*, 120. See Rousseau, *The Social Contract*, Book III, chap. VI: "The best kings want to be wicked if they wish, without ceasing to be masters. . . . First of all their personal interest is that the people be weak, miserable and that they never be able to resist them," *Du Contrat social*, Edited with an Introduction and Notes by Ronald Grimsley (Oxford, 1972), 168. Bossuet, on the other hand, had argued: "Government is established to free all men from all oppression and all violence, as had been often demonstrated. And that is what makes a state of perfect liberty: at bottom there is nothing less free than anarchy, which removes from men all legitimate pretention and knows no other right than that of force." Bossuet, *Politique tirée des propres paroles de l'Écriture sainte*, 293.

17. *Examen des principes*, 79.

18. Ibid., 79–80. For Bossuet on fundamental laws, see *Politique tirée des propres paroles*, 28.

19. Ibid., 80–81; Paul H. Beik, *The French Revolution Seen from the Right: Social Theories in Motion, 1789–1799* (Philadelphia, 1956), 102–3; Bossuet, *Politique tirée des propres paroles*, 19, 201.

20. *Examen des principes*, 81.

21. Ibid., 85; Bossuet, *Politique tirée des propres paroles*, 90.

22. See especially 129–132, 134, 136.

23. *Deféense de l'ordre social*, 38.

24. Ibid., 60–61.

25. Cited also in *Examen des principes*, 80.

26. *Défense de l'ordre social*, 136.

27. Ibid., 143.

28. Ibid., 61–62, 66.

29. Ibid., 79–80.

30. Ibid., 84. The only reference I can find that might possibly support this assertion is the following from *The Social Contract*: "all peoples have a kind of centrifugal force, by which they continually act against each other, and tend to advance themselves at the expense of their neighbors, like the vortices of Descartes," *Du Contrat social* (Oxford, 1972), Book II, chap. IX, 145.

31. *Défense de l'ordre social*, 91.

32. Ibid., 92.

33. *Examen des principes*, 88.

34. *Examen des principes*, 88–90; Bossuet, *Politique tirée des propres paroles*, 64–65.

35. *Examen des principes*, 91–92; *Défense de l'ordre social*, 150; Bossuet, *Politique tirée des propres paroles*, 70–71, 73–79.

36. *Defénse de l'ordre social*, 144, 148, 152. Bossuet said: "God, who bridles the waves of the sea, is the only one who can yoke the unmanageable disposition of the peoples," *Politique tirée des propres paroles*, 272.

37. The last statement seems an obvious reference to Napoleon or a figure like him. *Défense de l'ordre social*, 260.

38. For examples of this myth in the royalist press, see William J. Murray, *The Right-Wing Press in the French Revolution: 1789–92* (Woodbridge, Eng., 1986), 252–53.

CHAPTER VII

The Royalist Press and the Directory

In the Directory the press was relatively free[1] and the right-wing press had a real opportunity to advance its views. On general matters it raised the salient question of why the war should continue, a question that had a lot of political resonance after three years of fighting affecting hundreds of thousands of French soldiers and their families.

But a great deal of its attention focused on the past. The press was still concerned with the origins of the French Revolution. It found the answer to France's problems in a return to religion, which it believed would bring the French together again. And it compared republican government unfavorably to the type of monarchy that had existed in the Old Regime. Republicans fed on disorder to advance their own ends, while monarchists brought unity and a sense of common purpose.

Much of its commentary concentrated on specific issues that arose in connection with the election of 1797, the first under the Directory. Royalists argued that in the campaign, true to their nature, republicans were artificially stirring up trouble in order to promote their cause. Nevertheless royalists did well in the returns, but then proved unable to close ranks and work together. Moreover they were preoccupied with the broader political divisions of the past. On both ends of the political spectrum there was fear, a desire for retribution, and an unwillingness to accept the electoral process and agree to a peaceful transfer of power. Monarchists were taken up with the Jacobin threat and viewed the Jacobins as a monolithic conspiratorial organization. In the months after the election results they also feared a military coup. In the face of these threats some of them expressed a willingness to resort to force.

The royalists emphasized the uncertainty and the peril of continuing the war.[2] On October 24, 1796, *La Quotidienne ou Feuille du Jour* raised the question of the purpose of the war. Was it to extend and promote the Revolution? Or was it simply to defend what already had been accomplished? It believed the government might not have a very good idea itself. But the questions needed answers because the fate of France and the destiny of Europe hung on the outcome:

whether there would be peace, whether political systems would survive, and whether French armies would be just or unjust. The answer would decide if French generals would become fomenters of rebellion and anarchy, if they would seek to turn conquered peoples against their princes and kings, and if the French would become the opponents of all non-revolutionary governments. If the government really wanted universal disorder, instead of regional pacification, there would be no end to the revolution, which would eventually drain France of its strength and leave it at the mercy of the first person who wanted to pick up the pieces.

La Quotidienne said that, misled by the model of the ancient Romans, the French were imposing laws wherever they went with the idea of subjecting the whole globe to a French constitution whose existence was doubtful and that probably would not last more than a few days. With benevolence on their lips and a sword in their hand, they were proceeding to proclaim a doctrine whose ideas were unclear and whose results were uncertain.[3]

The picture presented by the well-named *Le Grondeur* in December of 1796 was bleak. It reported that not only was the war going on, but that the French armies were in trouble. Domestically the social fabric was weakening, and the economy was in a state of decay. There was unrestrained luxury, immorality, and scandal in one corner; elsewhere there was suffering, anguish, and extreme poverty. Robbery was common. Politically the factions intrigued to maintain their rule, while writers courageously kept on eye on them and sought to restrain them. The weak goverment preferred to instill fear in honest people rather than to support them. Most people wanted peace, which alone could restore order, but some called for the war to go on.[4]

How had the French people gotten themselves into such a plight? *Le Véridique* answered that it was the fault of the philosophes, "this false and vain philosophy that seduced the kings it was going to dethrone, the peoples it was to enchain, that sneaked to the foot of the altars it overthrew . . . that removed the fear from crime and the hope from virtue, that shook the institutions bound to the foundations of states . . . that rendered piety ridiculous, the distinction between good and evil problematic."[5]

La Quotidienne, however, believed the problem went back to the essence of French character. Since the days of Julius Caesar the French had always been "restless, capricious, carried away by the passions of the moment, imitators of everything, tired of everything. . . ."[6] They had always been changeable and uncertain. Their only constant trait was that they always had to be stirred up.

But it predicted that when the revolutionary fires had burned themselves out; when the true ideas of property and liberty came back; when people realized that they did not always have to engage in war; when religion, the only brake on the powerful and the only consolation of the weak, was able to recall the oppressors and the oppressed to obedience, then France, which had been weakened by a long illness, might begin to recover and come back to life.[7]

In the same year, 1797, a tract written by Nicolas Sourdat (1745–1810), *Les Véritables auteurs de la Révolution de France*, sought to explain the origins of the French Revolution and pointed the finger directly at the Protestants. According to Sourdat the Revolution resulted from a plot by the Calvinists against religion and against the throne, which began with the work of John Calvin himself. And it was precipitated by a Protestant, Jacques Necker, when he doubled the representation of the Third Estate. Then the deputies were able to lay the foundations and prepare for the success of the Revolution.[8]

By the time of the reign of Louis XVI, Sourdat found the Calvinists engaged in a conspiracy with the Jansenists, the philosophes, and the Freemasons, an alliance that by now had become familiar in royalist literature. But it was the Protestants who played the leading role in the Revolution. They dominated the discussion whenever they had an interest in the matter at hand. And it was Calvinist proposals that came out of the revolutionary assemblies. Calvinists sparked the revolt and moved to get rid of anything that they did not like. Eventually the Calvinists imposed such a reign of terror that no one was able to stop them.[9]

In February of 1797, *La Quotidienne* published an article on different forms of government. It said the Revolution had shown that in times of danger the authority of the various republican governments grew and that the most extreme crises led to tyranny. Republican government was made up of a number of different wills, but in times of trouble they united and formed a powerful government. In a monarchy, on the other hand, there was always one will and no need for outside stimulus.

So the royalist attack on the Convention on 13 vendémiaire 1795 actually had the effect of re-establishing its authority. Similarly the Babeuf conspiracy gave a big boost to the Directory. With a few more conspiracies the government could set up a tyranny. Experience showed that the sedition was always put down and served only to provide the republicans with the means to crush the people. It was clear that the government played up conspiracies so it could profit from them. Actually what it feared was tranquility much more than turmoil. If there weren't any plotters, it would have to have to hire actors to play that role.[10]

But the main thing capturing the attention of the royalist press was the election of March 1797, which would fill the seats of one-third of the legislature. In December of 1796, *La Quotidienne* announced that the approaching election frightened the revolutionaries because they realized that a new third, added to those already present in the legislature, could restrict their power and might lead to their overthrow. Clearly the new deputies could end the current misery.

So, according to this paper, in a desperate atttempt to save themselves, the radicals were stirring up trouble in the departments, persecuting priests, intimidating people, calling for the émigrés to return, menacing the rich, courting the poor, assassinating messengers, and then blaming the priests, the émigrés, and the Chouans for the trouble they had fomented themselves.

La Quotidienne said that, given this threat and because the Council of Five Hundred was such a hotbed of radicalism, all one could do was to turn to the Council of Ancients for support. It was up to the Council of Ancients, which already had rejected so many radical measures, to resist all the proposals designed to disrupt the election, either by delaying the primary assemblies or by presenting them with revolutionary propositions.

La Quotidienne closed by asserting that, while one might adopt an attitude of resignation in face of the mounting dangers and recognize that the challenges perhaps came from an angry God who was seeking to punish his people for their wickedness, as citizens one should join right-thinking leaders to resist the forces of darkness and make them feel some of the suffering that they had imposed on others.[11]

On March 10, 1797, the royal pretender, the comte de Provence, issued a Royal Declaration that sought to influence the approaching elections. The Declaration of 1797 praised the traditional constitution of France and claimed that it was opposed to anarchy, despotism, and the kind of government that existed at the end of the Old Regime. Furthermore the Declaration acknowledged that the old constitution was "susceptible to new degrees of perfectioning."

On other matters the emphasis had also changed. There was not much attention paid to the restoration of the three orders and the parlements. Instead the comte de Provence said he would listen to the wishes of the people as he went about correcting all the old abuses. Moreover he offered a full political amnesty and promised that he would allow no private acts of vengeance. In the upcoming election he urged Frenchmen to reject Jacobin extremists. And he promised to work for a political solution by peaceful means, one in which all those who believed in peace and order might join.

Though this declaration did not demonstrate that the pretender was willing to give up any of his old political aspirations, it did endorse the idea of peaceful change. The document was sufficiently ambiguous to make constitutional monarchists hope that the comte de Provence would eventually make genuine political concessions and to make ultraroyalists believe that he would not give up anything they considered essential. The purpose was to allay the fears that France had about him and to attract as many from the Center and the Right as possible for a united stand against the Left. This kind of juggling, however, was very difficult. References to the restoration of "holy religion" and "paternal government," for example, were enough to make some moderate royalists wonder whether the Bourbons were still out of touch.[12]

In the midst of the legislative election, which took place March 20–31, 1797, the *Actes des Apôtres et des Martyrs* of the comte Barruel-Beauvert said that the oath affirming hatred of royalty required by the Directory for those who participated in the electoral assemblies was illegal. Still one should not have any trouble agreeing to this pledge because one had previously been required to promise loyalty to the royal constitution of 1791, then to the anarchical constitution of 1793, and finally to the republican constitution of the Directory. None of these oaths meant anything.[13]

As it turned out the election of 1797 represented a defeat for the Directory. The newly elected deputies, added to those elected in 1795, produced a majority that was not well disposed to the Republic.[14] William Wickham, the British representative at Berne, estimated that the two houses together had more than 200 dependable royalists, about 200 definite republicans, and a large group of about 300 independents. So the Directory could not count on a republican majority, although there was not a royalist one either.[15]

The main problem of the opposition to the Directory was lack of unity. In the first place the monarchists were divided amongst themselves: many thought that the brothers of Louis XVI, the comte de Provence and the comte d'Artois, should retire in favor of Artois' son, the duc d'Angoulême. And they could not agree on what limitations, if any, to place on a restored monarch. Second, independent deputies were dismayed at the royalist ties to England, France's enemy, at the demands of the royalist extremists, and at the earlier policy statements of the comte de Provence. Furthermore the opposition had neither discipline nor effective tactical leadership. Some monarchists, who despaired of winning control peacefully, made plans for a *coup d'état* and then kept postponing it because they were unable to carry it out.[16]

After the election *Le Véridique* characterized the winners as men who understood the Revolution and always held themselves apart from it. They were men who wanted peace and tranquility, the return of order, the abolition of injustice, the complete healing of the wounds of the nation, and the destruction of all the revolutionary institutions. They wanted peace with foreign powers, union within, maintenance of authority within its constitutional limits, improvement of the constitution, payment of state debts, help for the poor, and tolerance for religion.[17]

In the aftermath of the election, the *Actes des Apôtres et des Martyrs* said that too much time was being spent on the imaginary concerns of revolutionaries who pretended to believe that they would not receive a pardon if the monarchy came back. These included politicians who had abused their power and journalists who had manipulated the news for their own personal gain. These groundless fears were nothing compared to the real evils that France had endured during the tyranny of people who came from the lowest dregs of society. But putting the question of a restoration aside, all people who had suffered from the revolutionary regime had the right to hope for a better order of things and should be free to express their ideas, which would not disturb public order but could help reestablish it on a lasting basis.[18]

By the middle of May the *Actes des Apôtres* complained that the March elections still had had no effect. The newly elected deputies had not been installed, the revolutionary laws were still in place, and the Jacobins had not been dismissed. Furthermore the Directory had not purged those responsible for the terror from the departments and had not brought prisoners to trial. In short, the constitution was not operating. And troops were coming into the area of Paris from all over France.[19]

In fact it warned of a continuing Jacobin threat. The Jacobins should not think that royalists were their dupes. Realization of their true nature came from having been and from still being their victims. Royalists knew that the Jacobins formed one body. They had their leaders, their treasurers, their secret agents, their correspondants, and their hack writers. They were the enemies of order and peace; they did not want an armistice, but only pillage and carnage. And they were preparing another revolution. Maybe at last these persecutors would answer for their crimes and atone for them. Maybe the only way to repress the assassins at Paris was to knock them in the head in the departments![20]

By June the *Actes des Apôtres* was somewhat more optimistic. It said some of the deputies elected in 1795 appeared to be willing to join with the royalists. And even some of the former members of the Convention gave indications that they favored moderation and justice. If all the moderate deputies worked with the newly elected ones, then the directors and the ministers would be unable to return to the terror. In fact, they had begun to fear that their former deeds would be punished. But the *Actes des Apôtres* preached toleration for all those who mended their ways and supported a new approach.[21]

In July the *Journal du Petit Gautier* said that things would get much better if the French would only take the comte de Provence back. It claimed it had received a letter from London indicating that there could be a general peace that was very favorable to France if the monarch returned. The *Journal du Petit Gautier* reported that George III, wishing to give Louis XVIII as glorious a return as Charles II, would give him a million pounds sterling worth of sugar and coffee to distribute to the people on his return. There need be no modification of the two chambers or of the directorate. The Constitution of 1795 would be preserved—the monarch would only be another guarantee of the constitution. The directorate, in this proposal, was the only constitutional council, without which the monarch could not achieve anything.[22]

By August, however, *Le Véridique* was more worried about an anti-royalist coup d'état. It wondered if the French would ever escape from the labyrinth of the Revolution. As soon as they got out of one crisis they were threatened by another. At present a group opposed to all social order (the Jacobins) were trying to seize control again and plunge France once more into anarchy. It wondered if enough blood had not flowed, if the country was not covered with enough ruins. It asked whether a people had ever worked as hard and as consistently to achieve their own fall.

Le Véridique said that it was in vain for the French to think that the Constitution of 1795 would assure them their rights and lead them to port. They clutched at this notion as a way to keep from drowning. The hope of a happier future made them forget their past. They had enjoyed a brief respite; commerce, industry, and the arts were reviving and attempting to restore France to its former glory. They awaited the day when peace would heal their wounds and when they could again enjoy the liberty for which they had paid such a heavy price.

But it was all an illusion. There were new storms on the horizon. Even the magistrates, who owed their place to the constitution and supposedly were anxious to defend it, were the first to violate it. Every day they made new attacks. They were overthrowing authorities named by the people and replacing them with men the people disapproved of. They were also declaring open war on national representatives (over whom they had no jurisdiction), including legislators whom the nation had chosen and who had their support.

Magistrates were surrounding themselves with men who were perverse and were favoring meetings that had been so disastrous in the past. They were also inviting the armies, which had given their blood for the defense of liberty, to help them oppress the people. They accused the most peaceful and orderly citizens of fomenting civil war, while they were organizing it themselves.

What was their goal? Did they hope for higher offices for themselves? Did they want to enslave the people? Was it really in their interest to help the enemies of the nation? If at present the Jacobins were asking for the support of the government in order to have a new uprising, once in power the first thing they would do would be to turn against the government. It was time, the author concluded, for magistrates to wake up to the dangers that threatened the nation and themselves.[23]

The next day the *Actes des Apôtres* sounded a rallying call for the defense of the royalist position. Now, it announced, was the time for action against the Jacobin threat. Those who timidly feared what would happen to the National Guard if it took a stand against tyranny needed to realize the situation was quite different from August 10, 1792, or even October 4–5, 1795.[24] In the first case the King did not want one drop of blood shed in his defense. Secondly the royalists had been opposed by the Convention, its committees, the Jacobins, the arsenal, the treasury, and their own lack of arms. But now they had a majority in the legislative body, and a minority in the directorate.[25] Moreover, as a result of their previous suffering, the royalists understood that they had to try everything and sacrifice everything now so that they did not fall again under the control of the Jacobins.[26]

In the meantime there was concern about Bonaparte. The *Accusateur public* said that if he had not fired on the royalists in October of 1795,[27] thereby massacring what the *Accusateur* described as peaceful inhabitants, he would not have become the great conqueror of Italy. He would not have criminally pronounced a discourse on July 14, 1797, that was shameful for France, the Councils, the Directory, and himself, and he would not have been able to put himself forward so notoriously. What the *Accusateur* expected from him was "ruin, carnage, and destruction."[28]

These fears, of course, were very much to the point because less than a month later in the *coup* of 18 fructidor (September 4, 1797), three of the directors who feared a royalist restoration invoked the help of Napoleon's deputy at Paris, General Augereau, to purge the legislature of the recently elected deputies. In a blow to the royalists, the rump legislature then annulled the election of almost 200 deputies, replaced two of the directors with dedicated revolutionaries, and deported a number of people. Furthermore laws against émigrés and non-juring clergy were renewed, people who returned illegally were threatened with the guillotine, and freedom of the press was suspended. Following this terrible setback, the royalists fled abroad or went underground, and the royalist press was muzzled.[29]

It was not until 1799 that the comte de Provence felt that he had a another chance to return to power. He himself was now more moderate and hence more attractive; he was moving toward to the position he would occupy in 1814. And he even acknowledged privately that it would be necessary to work with people who had participated in the Revolution. But he did not make any public declarations to this effect nor any promises. Hence he did not win much public support in France at this time. Among émigrés, however, his position was stronger. With the young duc d'Orléans compromised by his role in the Revolution and currently off on a trip to America, the comte de Provence seemed the logical candidate if there were a restoration.[30]

The same year marks the temporary revival of the royalist press. Commenting on the leftist coup of prairial (June 18, 1799), the *Feuille du Jour* said ironically that it produced most fortunate effects. It had pulled France out of the lethargy into which it had fallen and thrown it into the turmoil of civil war. It had replaced one sickness with another. Wanting the sick person to feel himself dying, it had administered cordials so that he could savor all the horrors of death. The law on hostages and the law on forced borrowing, which served to rearm the Jacobins, had been a tremendous success.[31]

On 13 fructidor VII (August 30, 1799), the *Feuille du Jour* evaluated the constitution of the Directory. It said it would be difficult to estimate its worth because it had constantly been violated; since its inception tyranny had reigned. Whereas the revolutionaries of 1793 had clearly set up their constitution as an empty idol to invoke on ceremonial occasions, those of 1795 thought it simpler to put their constitution in place and then govern as they would under a child king (though few regencies were as stormy and as disordered as this one). This constitution was finally declared of age on 30 prairial (June 18, 1799). But from the first moment of its so-called majority, the ministers smothered its voice, grabbed the scepter from its hands, and replaced it with the toys of childhood. Perhaps the regime would always function in this manner. If so perhaps one should fear one of the revolutions that occur under weak princes. "Weakness led the French monarchy to the edge of the abyss and delivered it into the hands of its enemies. . . ." The constitution of the Directory might expect the same fate.

The oppressed reached out for its protection, but there was no response. The constitution resembled an idol that lacked both eyes and ears. Offerings and prayers had no effect on it. Eventually one came to the conclusion that it was a powerless god who could offer no support.

People should respect a constitution, but they could do so only if they felt its benefits. If instead there were empty promises and no follow-through, then the constitution would be consigned to the scrap heap of history along with other myths that were useful to the ambitious, but disastrous to the welfare of the nations.[32]

The next issue focused on what one should do to establish true concord in France in the period after 30 prairial VII. Although the legislature had recently tried to return to the terror, the *Feuille du Jour* claimed that the evidence indicated one could not save the State except by peaceful means. The French were no longer willing to submit to the bloody yoke of 1793. Conflicts between parties, while perhaps useful at the beginning of the republic, now could have only disastrous consequences. Unity was the only way to salvation.[33]

Any such reunion of spirits would be very difficult because French politics had tended to produce different parties, to promote divisions, to increase discontent, to invent groups to express hatred, and to throw up obstructions of all kinds between the members of the citizen body. Instead of trying to forget about the Old Regime, the French had used those memories as a fertile source of conflict. As if the Revolution had not produced enough dissension itself, the revolutionaries dragged the nobles from their tombs so they could proscribe them. And then they established revolutionary cults, devoted to the furies, that outraged justice and were another fruitful source of discord.

The *Feuille du Jour* asked if the measures proposed by Briot[34] at the Council of Five Hundred—the abolition of the revolutionary festivals and the closing of the list of émigrés—were enough to end the divisions? It replied that it was certainly time to respond to the public clamor to close the proscription list, and it would be nice not to have to celebrate royalist defeats. But what difference would it make if the legislature cast aside one revolutionary decree in order to enact a worse one, such as the law on hostages, and if the prisons were opened up, as they were under the Convention, to consume the innocent. What in fact was needed was not so much symbolic measures, but substantive ones that would restore justice for all.

For example, it wasn't enough just to stop adding people to the proscription list. What about examining fairly the names of those already there, including people who had never left France? And what about the fate of people unfairly languishing in prison? How could one embrace unity when most of the members of the legislature stood ready to violate the constitution and the rights of man?

One should not rest content with half-way measures, the *Feuille du Jour* concluded. The proposals of Briot had opened the door of hope. When word of them spread throughout the country they could serve to calm the waters. But one should not be satisfied with a momentary effect and remain unwilling to enact other necessary measures. Once deceived, hope would turn into furious despair. Then the abolition of a few festivals would be regarded as an act of hypocrisy that would make tyranny even harder to bear. The legislature should not be afraid to embark on a completely new approach. It should repeal all the repressive laws passed since 30 prairial, especially the law on hostages. By so doing it would promote harmony and demonstrate that it could still respond to the voice of justice and humanity.[35] This article seems to raise more practical difficulties than it solves. It does recognize that the thorough program of reconciliation proposed would have to overcome the many political divisions of the past. But its idealistic program seriously underestimated the obstacles at that time. It followed the leftist coup of 30 prairial, after which neither the legislature nor the directorate was sympathetic to the Right. It came on the heels of French military defeats, which tended to promote a need for unity, not diversity, and made republican leaders look on royalists as suspects if not traitors. And then the royalists had contributed to this feeling by their uprising of August 5–25, which had just been put down when the article was printed. Furthermore this piece contained implicit threats of future uprisings if its terms were not met. The French certainly needed to come together. Whether they could do so in the late summer of 1799 remains doubtful.

Two days later this journal embarked on a refutation of some of the ideas of Rousseau. True politics, it maintained, should be based on experience. Missing the irony in its insistence on a theoretical position before, it now insisted that politicians should follow actual facts and not imaginary theories. For example, the *Social Contract* began with the statement: "Man is born free and everywhere he is in chains." Just because they found this assertion at the beginning of the book, many people accepted it as a scientific principle. Nevertheless it was entirely false. How could man be free at birth when his ignorance and his weakness made him completely dependent on those around him? And how could he be in chains after his intellectual and physical development and when in many societies he had learned to recognize truth and to practice virtue, traits that made him truly free? So we have here the conservative argument that people had to be civilized, and they needed strong institutions, such as absolute monarchy and the Catholic Church, to help them become so.

All republics, this article went on, were born in the midst of resistance and continued in the midst of disturbances. Montesquieu, Rousseau, and Mably, according to this account, argued that this agitation was a fundamental principle of republican government, which confused the movement necessary to produce and maintain its life with the agitation that destroyed it. It would be important to find out if such resistance was endemic to certain forms of government, and hence perpetual obstacles to man's perfectibility and happiness, or if it came from the evil of certain men. Rousseau said: "If the legislator makes a mistake in his objective and establishes a principle different from that which springs from the nature of things, the state will not cease from agitation until it is destroyed or changed and invincible nature has resumed its control."[36] But Rousseau mistook the native state of man for the natural state, the savage stage for the civil stage that worked for the perfectioning of intelligent human beings.

So the author proposed the following questions for politicians:

1. To find out if the problems of republics were part of their nature or were only caused by individual passions.

2. To discover whether power divided men only because it could not be shared.

3. To find the connection between the above propositions and whether the solution of the second would resolve the first.

The author concluded that the preservation of human beings called for prompt answers to these questions. The answers would lead to human happiness and to peace.[37]

A month later this paper presented an argument against the separation of powers. Power, it maintained, was metaphysically and physically indivisible. In fact it was necessary for one person to dominate wherever people were gathered together for their protection. Such was the case whether one found the origin of society in the family, which one man controlled by nature, or in a convention, as the philosophes would have it, where one person played the leading role by necessity. If a group was armed, one individual had to lead it. If it deliberated, one had to persuade it. Otherwise there would be division in the army and confusion in the assembly.

In a monarchy one person had power and that person never died. In a republic, however, several individuals held power in turn. That was the great difference between these forms of government. A legislative assembly was really a lottery, where power was up for grabs at each deliberation, so that power was really divided here too.

The separation and the balance of power was the great mistake of Montesquieu and the idle fancy of modern politicians. Supposedly the legislature expressed its wish and the executive carried it out. But if this were true then the executive was not a separate and equal power, but merely the agent of the legislature. So even in this example there weren't two powers with a real equilibrium between them, but only one.

Of course one could maintain that those seeking a balance did not ask for more and that the mistake lay, not in their system, but in its description. What they wanted to do, one could argue, was to limit power and its agents to their rightful place. But this is not at all what Montesquieu and his followers thought they found in the English constitution, where they believed there was a separation and a balance of powers. They said the legislative power was not independent because the king could refuse to approve acts of Parliament. Similarly Parliament, by withholding subsidies, could prevent the king from carrying out his will. What they were talking about was not just limiting power, but balancing it.

People who were searching for this solution were looking for an absurdity because such an equilibrium was contrary to the nature of society and something that could not be found. Because they were trying to find it there would be struggle, discord, and eventually anarchy. And in their effort to limit absolute power they would fall under the sway of an arbitrary regime. This imaginary equilibrium would cause England to fall, as it had the French monarchy when the parlements tried to balance their power with that of the king, and it would lead to the collapse of the French republic, where different branches were attempting to balance their power.

Honors, credit, favor, and wealth could be shared. Those were the accessories of power. But power itself was one and indivisible, a seamless tunic that the soldiers drew by lot. In every society undergoing a revolution the bloody struggle for power began with the scribes and the doctors, and was decided between the armies. That, the author concluded, was where France was at that time.[38]

This case against the balance of power seems to place excessive emphasis on the need for leadership of any group by one person. According to it any other approach was a violation of the scheme of nature. Furthermore it seems unable to even conceive of the possibility of a system of checks and balances. It makes the theory of French absolutism the standard to which everything else had to conform. Moreover while one can argue that the English constitution did not really operate according to Montesquieu's neat categories, the author of this piece does not appreciate the power-sharing that had evolved in England to produce a system that one could describe as much more stable and viable than anything the French had developed. Similarly the notion that any attempt to balance power would necessarily lead to arbitrary rule seems untenable.

But in spite of his à priori approach the author has some salient observations. There is the notion that the Old Regime fell because the parlements tried to get more power, a disputable point, but one that contains in embryo the idea of an aristocratic resurgence, which has had considerable influence in modern historiography. Clearly the author put his money on the king and expected the aristocrats to play a subordinate role. And, though one could argue with how the author reached his conclusion, this assessment of the contemporary political scene, one month before Napoleon's coup, was right on target.

This column took the offensive against Montesquieu again a few weeks later. It said that one of the most fanciful chapters of *Spirit of the Laws* was the one in which Montesquieu described the mechanism of the English government, as if it were a machine of physics, without realizing that the highly lauded equilibrium was actually being destroyed by corruption and venality. He thus contributed to an English craze that debased France and stole from it the approval it had always enjoyed. This infatuation for English ways was the source of the greatest misfortunes for France. The Revolution began with a quest for English liberty, but that lasted no longer than any other fad.

France wanted its own form of freedom, and the English, who thought France should follow blindly, were offended that it slipped the yoke and launched its own republic. Under the Jacobins it became fashionable to abuse the English system. But in spite of French criticism, the English seemed to maintain the strength of their system, as if to defy the French. The British monarchy even managed to turn the new principles to its advantage. While France was spreading liberty, the British were making new conquests for their commerce. At the present time, while France was fighting for glory, they were concentrating on their own interests and their own affairs. France was squandering its blood and its resources for misguided principles; England was gathering in the gold and silver of the universe and using them against France.

Returning to Montesquieu, the writer asserted that he addressed his remarks only to the mind. He was neither an orator nor an enthusiast—he did not speak to the heart. His reason confounded fanatics. So after the Revolution his reputation fell dramatically. Since he described despotism in such unfavorable terms, he came to be considered almost a counter-revolutionary. Praise then shifted to Rousseau, which demonstrated that opinion was both unjust and foolish, because Rousseau was "perhaps the most fearless and the most determined counter-revolutionary that ever existed."[39]

This author said that when he went into the French legislature and saw a bust of the author of the *Social Contract*, he thought to himself: there is the man who wrote that a representative system of government was a vestige of the barbarian era,[40] that no one could represent the will of a nation,[41] that people with representatives were slaves,[42] that democracy could only exist in a company of gods,[43] and that if people could not exercise power directly it would be better to forget about liberty since one tyrant would be better than several.[44] Such opinions, if uttered during the Revolution, would have been regarded as political blasphemy and their spokesmen subject to prison or the guillotine. So Rousseau's bust was presiding over representatives whom he had disparaged. It was like a picture that put the devil in heaven. This inconsistency led one to believe that there were many people who pretended to be learned, who needed to learn how to read.[45]

Then followed Napoleon's coup of brumaire (November 10, 1799). The response of the *Courrier universel* was favorable. Less than a month later it saluted 18 brumaire for delivering France from the hysteria of the republicans. It reported that a constitution was carefully being prepared that would correct the mistakes of the past ten years.[46] It maintained that the more that constitution got away from the principles of the French Revolution, the more it would approach the true spirit of France. In the current situation it believed the government that could do the best job of repressing license would be the one that most favored liberty.[47]

A few days later the same paper thought it saw "the dawn of good sense and of reason" on the political scene after a long period of darkness and degradation. In fact it found the disorders of the late eighteenth century comparable to the chaos of the barbarian era. The new government wanted to promote reason, protect private property, eliminate the fantasy of equality, and move toward monarchical principles.[48]

On January 3, 1800, it compared Napoleon as a general to the Emperor Trajan, but said Napoleon had a much better understanding of liberty and hence would do a much better job politically. And it remarked with pleasure that 18 brumaire was the last revolution the republic would have to endure.[49] The next day, while ostensibly discussing Julius Caesar, the *Courrier universel* offered Bonaparte unstinting praise: "Brave, clement, liberal, a great captain, a great statesman, eloquent, a good father, a devoted friend, a generous enemy, breathing only for glory, and seeking it only in the honor of being the first artisan of his country's prosperity. . . ."[50]

About a week after that, however, a note of caution crept in, and the paper printed a column that expressed concern that the Revolution might in fact not be over. After all laws that were supposed to end, the Revolution still had revolutionary elements. Furthermore the government was still making a distinction between those who had been condemned and those deported. Why were some allowed to return and others still excluded? Moreover because of their political or religious views, some were still subject to police surveillance. And people who had never left France were still branded as émigrés. Also all the positions in the government were filled with people who had been deeply involved in the Revolution, men who had bent to whatever wind was blowing at the time and who might well return to their former revolutionary habits. All of the current social structure rested on the life of a single man; what violence might ensue if something happened to him! So the Revolution was like a terrible disease that had spread throughout the country and from which France still had to recover.[51]

Finally this journal expressed its approval of the legislative arrangement in the constitution of the new Consulate, with a Tribunate that could discuss but not vote and a Legislative Body that could vote but not discuss. It especially liked the rules for the Tribunate, which it thought would put an end to the effects of the rhetorical excesses of the past. While the tribunes could talk their heads off, if they got carried away no one would be affected.[52]

Most domestic royalists accepted the new order and saw the *coup* as directed against the Jacobins: the new government ordered the exile of some Jacobins, arrested others, and repealed some revolutionary decrees. In fact some royalists saw in Napoleon a General Monk, who would lead the way to a restoration of the monarchy. Bonaparte thought he could use royalist ideas to support his regime. Moreover he tried to get the approval of conservative ideologues, such as Louis de Bonald, whose arguments for political absolutism accorded so well with Napoleon's own political practice. Those royalist writers who continued to oppose him did so on the grounds that he was a foreigner or that he was tyrannical.[53]

Between 1795 and 1797, and again in 1799, the royalist press had a great deal of freedom and a real chance to present its views. At a time when there was a possibility of peace, it used that opportunity to raise the important question of why the war should continue; it pressed the government to spell out what France's specific objectives were. It spoke out against French imperialism and also against the imperialism of English political principles, particularly the idea of separation of powers as interpreted by Montesquieu. In the process royalist newspapers were fashioning what was to become a conservative position that nations had different historical traditions and no nation had the right to impose its approach on others. Furthermore the royalists argued that French principles themselves were unclear, uncertain, and unlikely to last. They concluded that while England was concentrating on its own best interests, France was involved in a wild goose chase for glory and for ill-advised principles that would drain its vitality and leave it prey to a military dictator. The right-wing press showed contempt for the Directory. It pointed to the disorder, the violence, and the unconstitutional rule that had marked republican government and offered its interpretation of the monarchical record as a contrast. And, in spite of critical remarks about him, the right-wing press tried to appropriate Rousseau for its cause and turn him into the champion of counter-revolution. So the royalist press sometimes served the useful function of an opposition forum, offering criticism and proposing alternatives.

But it seems excessively preoccupied with the past and hence unable to address current developments effectively. It was still concerned with the origins of the French Revolution. It had a simplistic view of the Jacobins; it was afraid of past foes and sought to crush them. Simultaneously it called for an end to terror and repression, and a return to peace and concord, and then seemed to underestimate the difficulties of such an approach during a time of domestic upheaval, military influence, and foreign war.

At the same time royalist periodicals did not present enough of a positive program, which is a reflection of a general royalist failure at this time. They seem more effective at preaching to the converted than at rallying new support.[54] Royalists tended to tell more what they were against than what they were for. This is a definite disadvantage if one is competing for support in the popular market place. One is reminded again of R. R. Palmer's characterization of the failure of the Old Regime as in part a failure of public relations.[55] They did not sufficiently emphasize that after ten years of revolution and seven of war, the monarchy might really restore peace and domestic tranquility.

Moreover although monarchists were willing to participate in the election of 1797, they were not willing to accept the results of the electoral process. Some of them wanted to resort to force, which of course created fear and a desire to use force on the part of the opposition. The Right and the Left were very good at scaring each other.

A reading of the royalist press at this time also shows a lack of royalist unity and an inability of the royalists to work with other groups who had reservations about the Directory. Granted that they had not had much political experience, their dogmatism and their factionalism stood in their way. Eventually the polarization between political extremes led to the *coup* of fructidor and then to 18 brumaire.

Their reaction to the latter event can only be described as short-sighted. They believed that Napoleon had rescued them from all their foes. Somehow they were able to equate the repression of license with the promotion of liberty. They welcomed the end of equality and managed to convince themselves that the Consulate would evolve in a monarchical direction. So their hatred of republicans led them to embrace a military dictator.[56]

NOTES

An earlier version of this chapter was given at the Western Society for French History in November of 1990. It is based in part on copies of newspapers communicated to me by Jeremy D. Popkin.

1. Especially until the coup of fructidor (September 4, 1797), and then again between June and November of 1799. Claude Bellanger, Jacques Godechot, Pierre Guiral, and Fernand Terrou, *Histoire générale de la presse française*, I (Paris, 1969), 543–44; Georges Lefèbvre, *The Directory* (New York, 1964), 198–99.

2. For a general discussion of this subject see Jeremy D. Popkin, *The Right-Wing Press in France, 1792–1800* (Chapel Hill, 1980), 154–56.

3. *La Quotidienne ou Feuille du Jour*, October 24, 1796. *La Quotidienne* continued its anti-war message in an article on May 7, 1797, Popkin, *The Right-Wing Press*, 136. On *La Quotidienne*, see *The Right-Wing Press*, 16–24, 136, 145. Popkin divided the royalist press into two groups. One "that dealt seriously with the problems of political institutions and put their faith in a restoration through the republican constitutionary machinery itself, and extremist papers that ignored such mundane considerations in favor of an unsparing atack on every aspect of the new order," Popkin, *The Right-Wing Press*, 9. Of the newspapers treated here, *La Quotidienne* and *Le Veridique* (*Feuille du Jour, Courrier universel*) belong to the former category; *Le Grondeur*, *Actes des Apôtres*, *Journal du Petit Gautier*, and *Accusateur publique* to the latter. Popkin, *The Right-Wing Press*, 184, nn. 12–13.

4. *Le Grondeur*, December 14, 1796.

5. *Le Véridique*, November 24, 1796, quoted from Popkin, *The Right-Wing Press*, 120. On *Le Véridique's* views see Popkin, *The Right-Wing Press*, 80, 136, 154, 171, 184 n. 12.

6. *La Quotidienne*, January 6, 1797.

7. Ibid.

8. [Nicolas Sourdat] *Les Véritables auteurs de la Révolution de France de 1789* ([Neuchâtel] 1797), 7, 41. Sourdat produced a 1790 pamphlet entitled *Les Champenois du rois* that was inserted in the *Act des Apôtres*, and he wrote on behalf of Louis XVI

during his imprisonment in 1792 and 1793. His name was inscribed on the list of émigrés in 1793 and taken off in 1800. L. G. Michaud, *Biographie universelle, ancienne et moderne, Supplemént,* 82 (Paris, 1849), 402.

9. Ibid., 451ff., 489.

10. *La Quotidienne,* February 3, 1797. *Le Véridique* said on 6 messidor V (June 24, 1797), that the struggle for power in republics had the unfortunate effect of involving the masses in political life. Popkin, *The Right-Wing Press,* 136.

11. *La Quotidienne,* December 2, 1796.

12. Walter Ronald Fryer, *Republic or Restoration in France? 1794–7. The Politics of French Royalism, With particular reference to the activities of A. B. J. d'André* (Manchester, 1965), 179–81; P. J. B. Buchez and P. C. Roux, *Histoire parlementaire de la révolution française,* XXXVII (Paris, 1838), 242–44; R. R. Palmer, *The Age of Democratic Revolution, A Political History of Europe and America, 1760–1800,* II (Princeton, 1964), 249.

13. *Actes des Apôtres,* March 26, 1797. On this newspaper see Claude Bellanger et al., eds., *Histoire générale de la presse française,* I, 528; René de Livois, *Histoire de la presse française,* I (Paris, 1965), 149–51. The *Actes des Apôtres* was edited by Antoine Joseph de Barruel-Beauvert, whom Popkin described as an "addlepated extremist," who "may well have had more impact than many of the tamer right-wing journalists . . .," Popkin, *The Right-Wing Press in France,* 48–49.

14. R. R. Palmer, *The Age of Democratic Revolution,* II, 256.

15. Walter Ronald Fryer, *Republic or Restoration in France,* 207.

16. R. R. Palmer, *Age,* II, 256–57; Fryer, *Republic or Restoration in FRance,* 208–9.

17. *Le Véridique ou Courrier universel,* April 21, 1797.

18. *Actes des Apôtres et des Martyrs,* April 30, 1797.

19. *Actes des Apôtres et des Martyrs,* May 14, 1797.

20. Ibid.

21. *Actes des Apôtres et des Martyrs,* June 18, 1797.

22. *Journal du Petit Gautier,* July 1, 1797.

23. *Le Véridique,* August 12, 1797. Georges Lefèbvre, on the other hand, presented quite a different picture. While recognizing that the Directory replaced some officials it considered suspect, he talked about the partiality of royalist tribunals and maintained the Directory did not do much against the royalists until August 23, when Carnot stepped down as the presiding officer. Only then did it move toward a coup d'état. Georges Lefèbvre, *La France sous le Directoire, 1795–1799,* Nouvelle édition (Paris, 1984), 418, 421–23.

24. The overthrow of the King and the crushing of a royalist plot, respectively.

25. As indicated before, this seems unlikely.

26. *Actes des Apôtres et des Martyrs,* August 13, 1797.

27. Thereby putting down the royalist uprising of vendémiaire, October 5, 1795.

28. *Accusateur publique,* August 7, 1797. On July 14, 1797, Napoleon said to his troops in Italy: "I know that you are deeply moved by the ills that threaten the Fatherland. . . . Mountains separate us from France: but you would cross them with all the swiftness of an eagle to uphold the constitution, defend liberty, and protect the government and the republic. . . . The moment when the royalists show themselves will be their last. . . . Let us swear by the shades of the heroes who died at our side for liberty, let us swear on our new banners, 'Total war against the enemies of the Republic and of

the Constitution of the Year III.'" J. M. Thompson, *Napoleon Bonaparte His Rise and Fall* (Oxford, 1952), 84. On the *Accusateur publique*, see Claude Bellanger et al., *Histoire générale de la presse française*, I, 526–27; Popkin, *The Right-Wing Press*, 9, 10, 14, 145. It was edited by J. T. Richer-Sérizy.

29. Georges Lefèbvre, *La France sous le Directoire, 1795–1799*, 429–33.

30. R. R. Palmer, *Age*, II, 552–53.

31. *Feuille du Jour, ou Courrier universel*, August 26, 1799. The law on hostages made the families of émigrés vouch for their behaviour and the law on forced borrowing imposed a compulsory loan on the rich. Martyn Lyons, *France Under the Directory* (New York, 1975), 226–27.

32. *Feuille du Jour*, August 30, 1799.

33. Government measures were taken in the face of the allied attacks on the French. There is a certain irony in the call here for peaceful means because royalists, hoping to profit from the allied attacks, had just launched (ca. August 5–25, 1799) an uprising, which proved unsuccessful. Denis Woronoff, *The Thermidorean Reaction and the Directory 1794–1799*, Translated by Julian Jackson (New York, 1984), 183–84.

34. Session of 12 fructidor VII (August 29, 1799), *Réimpression de L'Ancien Moniteur*, 29 (1863), 17 fructidor VII, 794–95.

35. *Feuille du Jour*, August 31, 1799.

36. Jean-Jacques Rousseau, *Du Contrat social*, Edited with an Introduction and Notes by Ronald Grimsley (Oxford, 1972), Book II, chap. XI, 150.

37. *Feuille du Jour*, September 2, 1799. Jeremy Popkin suspected that the vicomte de Bonald may have written some of the major theoretical articles for this newspaper at this time. Popkin, *The Right-Wing Press in France*, 129, n. 19. If so, he may have been the author of this and the following one.

38. *Courrier universel* (previously *Feuille du Jour*), October 9, 1799.

39. The attempt to capture Rousseau for the counter-revolutionary cause was a common effort of the Right. See Gordon H. McNeil, "The Anti-Revolutionary Rousseau," *The American Historical Review*, LVIII (July, 1953), 808–23. Jeremy Popkin cites another example in the royalist press in 1797, Popkin, *The Right-Wing Press*, 122.

40. *Du Contrat social*, Grimsley ed., Book III, chap. XV, 190.

41. *Du Contrat social*, Book III, chap. XV, 190–91.

42. Ibid., 191–92.

43. Ibid., chapter IV, 165.

44. I can find no place where Rousseau says precisely that. It of course is an extension of the passage referred to in footnote 71. Rousseau does say: "In effect, I believe that I can lay down the principle that when the functions of government are shared among several magistrates, sooner or later the smallest number will acquire the greatest authority, if only because of the facility to expedite affairs that they naturally bring to the task." Ibid., 164.

45. *Courrier universel*, October 21, 1799.

46. The constitution of the Consulate went into operation on December 25, 1799.

47. *Courrier universel*, December 7, 1799.

48. *Courrier universel*, December 12, 1799.

49. *Courrier universel*, January 3, 1800.

50. Quoted from Popkin, *The Right-Wing Press*, 147.

51. *Courrier universel*, January ll, 1800.

52. *Courrier universel*, January 13, 1800.

53. Georges Lefèbvre, *Napoléon*, Sixième édition (Paris, 1969), 74; Jeremy Popkin, *The Right-Wing Press*, 147.

54. This is in line with the evidence of Jeremy Popkin that the right-wing press often did more to express existing opinion than to control it. Popkin, *The Right-Wing Press*, 82–83.

55. R. R. Palmer, *The Age of Democratic Revolution, A Political History of Europe and America, 1760–1800*, I (Princeton, 1959), 86–87.

56. On January 7, 1800, Napoleon reduced the number of Paris newspapers to thirteen and later to four. Only two right-wing papers survived: the *Journal des Débats* and the *Publicisite*. Popkin, *The Right-Wing Press*, 171.

CHAPTER VIII

Royalist Historiography and Royalist Political Thought

Royalists made basic contributions in explaining the causes of the Revolution and in elaborating their own political principles. In the area of thought it cannot be said that the Bourbons and their supporters learned nothing and forgot nothing.

Though the Revolution involved catastrophic change from their point of view, they sometimes spent more time trying to figure out why it had taken place than in coming up with a program to cope with it. And in some of their early explanations, they opted for the easy way out: the Old Regime was alright, but it had been subverted by a fiendish outside conspiracy of philosophes, Protestants, Jansenists, and others.

Then royalists moved beyond that approach a bit, though still focusing on scapegoats, by claiming the Revolution was the fault of the kings' ministers. The kings were good rulers, but they received bad advice. There was too much turnover in the ministries and too many ministers who were inept. The obvious conclusion, though not one made by the royalists, was that these faults were the responsibility of the kings. The finance ministers, who were the focal point of the problem, were worst of all. There was continual turnover and, instead of concentrating on long-range solutions, ministers played with short-term measures that would keep them going until it was time to bail out.[1]

But eventually some right-wing historians recognized that one could not stop with royal agents, but must go on to assign responsibility to the kings themselves. It was relatively easy to point the finger at Louis XV. He ruled a long time, was noted for his disinterest in administrative details and his preoccupation with his mistresses, and many considered the reforms carried out by Maupeou at the end of his reign "despotic." But to criticize Louis XVI, whom many royalists considered a martyr, was another matter. Nevertheless as early as 1793 the comte de Ferrand cited the lack of effective reform during the reign of Louis XVI. Ferrand believed Louis XVI's government could have handled the situation by itself, and that revealing the extent of the financial problems and convening the Notables and the Estates-General were big mistakes.[2] But by 1800, Bertrand de Moleville had no qualms about elaborating all the mistakes and the missed opportunities of this reign.[3]

Early in the Revolution some royalists broadened their scope beyond individual scapegoats to cite the role played by public opinion. As early as 1789, Antoine Rivarol said the Old Regime failed partly because it failed to employ influential writers.[4] In 1794, Antoine Sabatier de Castres went so far as to assert that the Revolution took place because of public opinion, which the monarchy had not controlled.[5] What we have here, though it has broader implications, I think is essentially an extension of the conspiracy theory of history. Previously it was the philosophes who were the problem. Now it becomes the uncontrolled writers in general. In both cases the Old Regime was all right: it was the writers who were wrong. And in both instances there is a recognition of the power of ideas and of opinion, but an exaggeration of it.

But royalists tackled some more fundamental causes, ones that had a lot of reverberation in the twentieth century. They were the ones who came up with the notion of an aristrocratic resurgence in the eighteenth century, which led to the Revolution. And some of them identified a middle class revolution behind it. Aristocrats feared displacement by the bourgeoisie, that wealth would replace the old order, that equality would undermine the old classes, and that a republic, led by the middle class, would take the place of the Old Regime.[6] Royalists were also remarkable for identifying another factor which has come into play in twentieth century history: the impact of the American Revolution on the French Revolution, which is related to their emphasis on the role of public opinion.

The right-wing also took up the question of how the French Revolution was able to succeed once it got started. Here the usual factors came into play: the weakness of Louis XIV, the evil designs of Necker, and the results of the Enlightenment. But by 1795, another factor was becoming obvious: the unwillingness or the inability of foreign kings to come to the effective aid of the French monarchy.[7]

So royalists began their explanations of the causes of the French Revolution with the conspiracy theory of history, which absolved the Old Regime of all responsibility and assigned it to villainous outside forces: the philosophes, the Protestants, the ministers, the court of Louis XVI. But some soon came to recognize that there were flaws and problems within the Old Regime itself, that Louis XVI, while saintly, was weak, that no one in the government moved effectively to control public opinion, that basic social factors were at work undermining the system, and that foreign kings often decided that it was advantageous to have a weak France and thus did little to stem the revolutionary tide. So their accounts became increasingly sophisticated, and hence they made an important contribution to the understanding of the causes of the Revolution.

But their main task was to examine their past principles and see if they should hold firm to them or make some changes so they could get back into power again. They had previously sought to defend royal power by citing the divine right of kings and by calling on historical tradition, the argument from prescription. They had also appropriated the utilitarian rationale of the philosophes and claimed that strong kings were the best reformers.

One of their first tasks during the Revolution was to justify the record of the Old Regime. What they did was to construct a myth that everything was all right under the Old Regime; there was peace, plenty, and order, which they then contrasted readily with the serious problems under the Revolution.

It should be said that some royalists really did not know what program to pursue, but believed that they should vigorously follow one course after another so that something would get done. This was especially the case with the right-wing journalist François Louis Suleau, who in turn called for constitutional change, tried to get Louis XVI moving, went over to the side of the émigrés for a time, predicted despotism for France, and eventually called for war and the victory of France's enemies.

But most of them were more consistent. Some still invoked the sanction of the divine right of kings. Others sought to buttress their position by calling upon the argument from prescription. And still others argued that one continued to need an elite, the only group trained and fit to handle the reins of government.

Royalists opposed the individualism implicit in the French Revolution and argued that the claims of society overrode those of the individual. They came up with the organic theory of history before Edmund Burke. As early as 1789 Chaillon de Jonville maintained: "New operations are only good when they are placed in some fashion at the side of the constitution, and take effect by degrees and bring a long and low perfection."[8] The abbé Du Voisin came to the same conclusion. Gradual change was the only way; otherwise the pillars supporting society would collapse, as they had in the French Revolution, and there would be chaos.[9]

Royalists also sought to make use of a utilitarian approach; kings were best because they governed best. As early as 1791 and 1792, they argued that a king could best maintain order and prosperity, solve internal social problems, and establish peace with foreign rulers. Jean Langlois added to this rationale by asserting that France had to have an absolute monarchy because it was a large country, with a large population, and it shared borders with equally strong states. So its govenment had to solve domestic problems and meet foreign challenges.[10] The abbé Du Voisin shared these views and then went off on his own tack: the French were so weak and so evil that they had to have strong rulers.[11] The problem with these arguments was that no one offered convincing evidence that kings had in fact ruled better.

Except for constitutional monarchists, one thing that most right-wing commentators were agreed on was opposition to the concept of separation of powers. According to Jean Thomas Langlois, it was absolutely unworkable for France. It would set France on a course toward factionalism, disorganization, civil war, foreign invasion, and political despotism.[12]

The abbé Du Voisin and other right-wingers favored established governments and gave subjects with complaints no effective means of redress. Du Voisin put the emphasis on order and neglected political accountability. He and other royalists did recognize that there were limits on the power of the king, particularly in the fundamental laws. Moreover he said that if the fundamental laws were broken people could demonstrate peacefully, but he gave them no other alternatives if peaceful means did not succeed.[13]

One of the main problems of royalist political thought was that it was willing to countenance war and domestic violence to defend and advance its position if necessary. This approach helped engender violence in its political opponents and eventually led to the overthrow of the King and the royalists. In 1792 royalists tried to use war to bolster the King's position and to destroy those who opposed him. And they used threats against their political foes at home. The result, of course, is well known.

By the time of the Directory, however, royalist opinion had mellowed. In 1796 the royalist newspaper *La Quotidienne* questioned the need for the war to go on. It argued that a continuing war would sap French strength and leave it prey to the first person who wanted to preside over the ruins.[14]

But on the domestic scene the Right never was able to give up violence entirely. In fact as early as the period of the National Assembly the Left and the Right used threats, retribution, and civil war against each other. Royalists were willing to take part in elections, but not to abide by the results. When things did not go their way, some of them advocated using force, which made the Left distrustful and more willing to use violence itself. The Right and the Left frightened, and then persecuted each other. Eventually the Right convinced themselves that Napoleon would protect them from their enemies. They accepted curbs on liberty, welcomed the end of equality, and deluded themselves into thinking that the Consulate would develop into a monarchy. Though they did not realize it, their hatred of the Left carried them to the doorstep of a dictator.

The Right was consistently opposed to French imperialism. The royalist newspaper *La Quotidienne* said that the French were falsely trying to follow the example of the ancient Romans, who had a viable civilization and a workable system of government. The French, on the other hand, were trying to impose a regime that was tenuous and ephemeral.[15] During the Directory the press also spoke out against what it saw as the imperialism of British political ideas, such as the separation of powers. What was going on here was the creation of a conservative position that no country should impose its system on another, an approach that went along with the organic theory of history and was one that had considerable political play in the nineteenth century. At the same time, during the Revolution French monarchists came to feel a considerable sense of solidarity with monarchists in other countries. They expected help from them, and they argued that monarchy as a whole would fall unless they all stuck together.

As early as 1789 what we have among these monarchists is the search for a new principle of political authority. Their old approach had been challenged and rejected. They, in turn, rejected the new ideas of the Left, which they felt ungrounded, foreign, godless, and temporary. What they did was to combine religion, morality, an organic sense of history, and a reformed monarchy in a new defense of the political and social order. This work was crucial in preparing them for the opportunities that presented themselves after the fall of Napoleon, by which time many people were tired of republican experiments and Napoleonic wars. So from the viewpoint of royalist political thought, the period of the French Revolution was not just a time of retreat and defeat; it was also a time of regrouping and renewal.

Nevertheless, at this time monarchists did not come up with a program that was positive enough. They criticized their foes, rather than presenting their program. They were better at addressing the converted than the unbelievers. Again we have again R. R. Palmer's idea of a failure of public relations. During the Old Regime royalists felt they did not need to stoop to compete in the marketplace of ideas. During the Revolution some of them identified this as a shortcoming, but they often failed to heed their own admonitions. They had a message that got lost: the monarchy could bring peace and might restore domestic harmony.

Also the royalists often were not effective politicians. Royalists were not united among themselves, and they could not work well with other groups. It is true that they lacked political experience, but they insisted on their own way and they divided into factions. They did not seem trustworthy, although their foes often did not either. Eventually the political impasse between Left and Right led to the use of force in the coups of the Directory and the final coup of Napoleon, which ended the chance for meaningful political representation for a generation.

NOTES

1. Gabriel Sénac de Meilhan, *Des principes et des causes de la Révolution en France*, 35.
2. comte de Ferrand, *Le Rétablissement de la monarchie*, 18–19.
3. Bertrand de Moleville, *Annals of the French Revolution*, I, Chap. I.
4. *Journal Politique-Nationale*, August 9, 1789, 4–5.
5. *Pensées et observations morales et politiques*, 170–71.
6. Gabriel Sénac de Meilhan, *Des principes et des causes de la Révolution en France*, 78–79, 81; *Du gouvernement, des moeurs, et des conditions en France*, 93–94, 128–29.
7. Ferrand, *Des Causes qui ont empêché la contre-révolution en France*, 65.
8. *Apologie de la constitution françoise*, I, 161.
9. *La France chrétienne, juste et vraiment libre*, 158–59.
10. *Des Gouvernements qui ne conviennent pas à la France* (1795), ll–12.
11. *Defénse de l'ordre sociale contre les principes de la Révolution françoise* (1801), 23, 233.

12. *Des Gouvernemens qui ne conviennent pas à la France*, 35–39.

13. *Examen des principes de la Révolution françoise* (1795); *Défense de l'ordre social* (1798, 1801).

14. *La Quotidienne ou Feuille du Jour*, October 24, 1796.

15. Ibid.

Bibliography

ROYALIST NEWSPAPERS

Accusateur public (1795–97)
Actes des Apôtres (1796–97)
L'Ami du Roi (June 1–November 5, 1790)
L'Ami du Roi, edited by Montjoie (June 1, 1790–August 10, 1792)
L'Ami du Roi, edited by abbé Royou (September 1, 1790–May 4, 1792)
Annales politiques, civiles et littéraires du dix-huitième siècle, edited by Linguet (1777–1780, 1783–1784, 1787–1792)
L'Aristarque français, Journal universel (1799–1800)
Gazette de Paris (1789–1792)
Le Grondeur (1796–1797)
Journal de M. Suleau (1791–1792)
Journal du Petit Gautier, Suite de celui de la Cour et de la Ville, interrompu le 10 août 1792 (1797)
Journal général (1791–1792)
Journal Général de la Cour et de la Ville (1789–1792)
Journal-Pie (1792)
Journal Politique-National (1789–1790)
La Quotidienne, ou Tableau de Paris, Bulletin Politique, Feuille du Jour (1792–1797)
Le Véridique, Courier du Jour, Feuille universelle, Feuille du Jour, Courrier universel (1796–1800)

PAMPHLETS

Adresse aux Français. N.p. [1791].
Agoult, Charles Constance d'. *Bon Dieu! qu'ils sont bêtes ces Français!* Paris, 1790.
______. *Ouvrex donc les yeux*. N.p., n.d.
______. *Principes et réflexions sur la constitution française*. N.p., n.d.
Allonville, comte Armand d'. *Lettres d'un royaliste à M. Malouet, du mardi 22 mai 1792*. Paris: Au Palais-Royal, 1792.

Antraigues, Emmanuel Louis Henri de Launey, comte d'. *Exposé de notre antique et seule légale constitution française, d'après nos loix fondamentales . . . en réponse aux observations de M. de Montlosier.* Paris, 1792.

[Antraigues, Emmanuel Louis Henri de Launay, comte d']. *Mémoire sur les États généraux, leurs droits, et la manière de la convoquer.* N.p., 1788.

______. *Point d'accommodement.* N.p., n.d.

Argenson, René Louis de Voyer, marquis d'. *Considérations sur le gouverement ancien et présent de la France.* Amsterdam [i.e. Paris]: chez M. Rey, 1765.

Auger, abbé Athanase. *Moyens d'assurer la révolution, d'en tirer le plus grand parti pour le bonheur et la prosperité de la France, avec une Adresse à l'Assemblée nationale; et les Réflexions sur le Pouvoir executif.* Paris: Garnery, An I.

Barruel, abbé Augustin de. *Histoire du clergé pendant la révolution françoise.* London: J. P. Coghlan, 1793.

______. *Mémoires pour servir à l'histore du jacobinisme.* Nouvelle édition revue et corrigée par l'auteur. 4 vols. Lyon: Pitrat, 1818–1819.

______. *Memoirs, illustrating the history of Jacobinism.* A translation from the French of the Abbé Barruel. 4 vols. London: T. Burton and Co., 1797–1799.

______. *Le patriote véridique, ou discours sur les vraies causes de la révolution actuelle.* Paris: Crapart, 1789.

______. *Question nationale sur l'autorité et sur les droits du peuple dans le gouvernement.* Paris: Crapart, 1791.

Barruel-Beauvert, comte Antoine Joseph de. *Première Collection du Journal royaliste, depuis le 16 mars 1792 jusques au 14 juin inclusivement (et depuis le 16 juin 1792 jusques au 9 août 1792).* Paris: Denne, n.d.

Bertrand de Moleville, Antoine François. *Annals of the French Revolution.* Translated by R. G. Dallas, Esq., from the original manuscript of the author, which has never been published. 4 vols. London: T. Cadell & W. Davies, 1800.

______. *Observations adressées a l'Assemblée des notables sur la composition des États Généraux et sur la forme la plus régulière de les convoquer.* N.p., n.d.

______. *Mémoires particuliers, pour survir à l'histoire de la fin du règne de Louis XVI.* 2 vols. Paris: L. G. Michaud, 1816.

______. *Private Memoirs Relative to the Last Year of the Reign of Lewis the Sixteenth, Late King of France.* Translated from the original manuscript of the author, which as never been published. 3 vols. London: A. Strahan, T. Cadell jun. and W. Davies, 1797.

______. *La Proclamation de Louis XVIII revue et corrigée.* N.p., n.d.

______. *Réflexions sur la Révolution de France; et sur les errors le plus généralement adoptées relativement à l'ancienne constitution de ce royaume, et au prétendu despotisme de son gouvernement.* London: Spilsburg, 1796.

______. *A Refutation of the Libel on the Memory of the late King of France*, published by Helen Maria Williams, under the title of Political and confidential correspondence of Lewis the Sixteenth. Translated from the original manuscript by R. C. Dallas. London: Cadell & Davies, 1804.

Bouquet, Pierre. *Lettres provincials, ou Examen impartial de l'origine, de la constitution, et des révolutions de la monarchie française.* The Hague: Le Neutre; Paris: Merlin, 1772.

Bouyon, abbé L. Bonnefoy de. *La constitution, ou La France telle qu'elle doit être*. Paris: Veuve Guillaume, 1790.

Calonne, Charles Alexandre de. *De l'état de la France, présent & à venir*. Londres: T. Spilsbury & Fils, October, 1790.

______. *De l'état de la France tel qu'il peut et qu'il doit être; Pour faire suite à l'État de la France présent et à venir. London, Paris, November, 1790.*

______. *Lettre adressée au Roi, par M. de Calonne, le 9 fevrier 1789*. London: T. Spilsbury, [1789].

______. *Seconde lettre adressée au Roi par M. de Calonne. Le 5 Avril 1789*. London: imp. de T. Spilsbury, n.d.

______. *Tableau de l'Europe en novembre 1795*. London: J. de Boffe, n.d.

[Chaillon de Jonville, Augustin Jean François]. *Apologie de la constitution françoise; ou Etats républicains et monarchiques, comparés dans les Histoires de Rome & de France*. 2 vols. N.p., 1789.

______. *La Révolution de France prophétisée, ainsi que ses causes infernales, des effets sinistres, et les suites hereuses, qui seront une restauration générale et une réforme complète de tous les abus en 1792. Suite de "La Révolution de France prophétisée. . . ."* 2 vols. Paris, 1791.

______. *Supplément à "La Révolution de France prophétisée."* Paris, 1791.

Condé, Louis Joseph, duc de Bourbon. *Louis-Joseph de Bourbon, prince de Condé, aux Français*. N.p., n.d.

Contre les horreurs du jour. A tous les vrais François par an Ami d l'Autel, du Trône et de la Patrie. N.p., 1791.

Délibération à prendre par le tiers état dans toutes les municipalités du royaume de France. N.p., November 1788.

Dubos, abbé Jean Baptiste. *Histoire critique de l'etablissement de la monarchie française*. Paris: Osmont, 1734.

______. *Histoire critique de la monarchie françoise dans les Gaules*. Nouvelle édition, revûe, corrigée & augmentée. 4 vols. Paris: chez Didot, 1742.

Du Voisin, Jean Baptiste. *Défense de l'ordre social, contre les principes de la révolution française*. Nouv. ed. Leipzig, 1801.

[Du Voisin, Jean Baptiste]. *Examen des principes de la Révolution françoise*. Wolfenbuttel, 1795.

______. *La France chrétienne, juste et vraiment libre*. N.p., 1789.

Ferrand, Antoine François Claude, comte de. *Des Causes qui ont empêché la contre-révolution en France, et Considérations sur la révolution sociale; suivies d'une notice sur Robespierre et des complices*. Bern: Em. Haller [1795].

______. *Considérations sur la révolution sociale*. London, 1794.

[Ferrand, Antoine François Claude, comte de]. *Lettres d'un commercant à un cultivateur sur les municipalités*. N.p., January 1790.

______. *Douze lettres d'un commerçant à un cultivateur sur les municipalités*. n.p. [1790].

______. *Nullité et despotisme de l'Assemblée prétendue nationale*. [Paris, 1790].

______. *Le Rétablissement de la monarchie*. N.p., September 1793.

François connoissez votre Roi. N.p., 1791.

[Goudar, Ange]. *L'autorité des rois de France est indépendante tout corps politique*. Amsterdam, 1788.

Langlois, Jean Thomas. *De la Souveraineté*. Paris: Richard, 1797.

______. *Des Gouvernemens qui ne conviennent pas à la France*. Paris: les marchands de nouveautés, 1795.

______. *Qu'est-ce qu'une Convention nationale?* . . . Paris, Debarle, 1795.

Lefranc, abbé Jacques François. *Conjuration contre la religion catholique et les souverains*. Paris: Lepetit, 1792.

[Lefranc, abbé Jacques François]. *Le voile levé pour les curieux ou le Secret de la Révolution révélé à l'aide de la franmaçonnerie*. N.p., n.d.

[Le Roy de Barincourt, D.]. *La Monarchie Parfaite, ou L'accord de l'autorité d'une Monarque avec la liberté de la Nation qu'il gouverne; Discours*. Geneva; Paris: chez Briand, 1789.

______. *Principe fondamentale du droit des souveraines*. 2 vols. Geneva, 1788.

Le Tellier, abbé François. *Observations philosophiques, théologiques, politiques, et historiques sur la Souveraineté du Gouvernement en général, & sur celle du Gouvernement Français en particulier*. Paris: Senneville, 1791.

[Linguet, Simon Nicolas Henri]. *Du plus heureux gouvernement, ou parallèle des constitutions politiques de l'Asie avec celles de l'Europe*. 2 vols. London, 1774.

______. *Lettres sur la Théorie de loix civiles* . . . Amsterdam, 1770.

______. *Théorie des loix civiles, ou Principes fondamentaux de la société*. 2 vols. London [i.e. Paris], 1767.

Louis XVIII. *Déclaration du Roi. Donné au moi de Juillet . . . 1795*. N.p., n.d.

______. *Lettre du roi Louis XVIII à M. Monnier, ex-président de la lre Assemblée constituante*. Bordeaux: impr. de F. Degréteau, [1878].

______. *Louis XVIII, aux français*. N.p., n.d.

Louis Stanislas Xavier et Charles Philippe. *Promulgation des sentiments des Princes, frères du Roi*. N.p., n.d.

Manière judicieuse et équitable d'envisager l'autorité. N.p., n.d.

Martin-Doisy, Félix, ed. *Manuscrit inédit de Louis XVIII, précédé d'un Examen de sa vie politique jusqu'à la Charte de 1814*. Paris: L. G. Michaud, 1839.

Montgaillard, Jean Gabriel Maurice Rocques, comte de. *L'An 1795, ou Conjectures sur les suites de la Révolution française*. Hamburg, 1795.

______. *État de la France au mois de mai, 1794*. London: E. Harlow, 1794.

[Montjoie, Christophe Félix Louis Ventre de la Touloubre]. *L'Ami du roi, almanach des honnêtes gens. Avec des prophètes pour chaque mois de l'année*. Paris, n.d.

______. *Éloge historique et funèbre de Louis XVIe du nom, roi de France et de Navarre*. Neuchâtel: Imprimeries royale, 1796.

Montyon, Antoine Jean Baptiste Robert Auget, baron de. *Rapport fait à sa majesté, Louis XVIII*. Constance, 1796.

[Moreau, Jacob Nicolas]. *Essai sur les bornes des connaissances humaines*. Lausanne; Paris: Mérigot, E. Onfroy, Barrois, 1784.

Moreau, Jacob Nicolas. *Exposé historique des administrations populaires, aux plus anciennes époques de notre monarchie; dans lequel on fait connoître leurs rapports & avec la puissance royale & avec la liberté de la nation*. Paris: Briand, 1789.

______. *Exposition et défense de notre constitution monarchique françoise, précédée de l'historique de toutes nos assemblées nationales; dans deux mémoires, ou l'on établit qu'il n'est aucun changement utile dans notre administration, dont cette constitution même ne nous présente les moyens*. Paris: Moutard, 1789.

______. *Leçons de morale, de politique et de droit publique, puisées dans l'histoire de notre monarchie. Ou nouveau plan d'étude de l'histoire de France. Rédigé par les ordres & d'après les vues de feu Monseigneur le Dauphin, pour l'instruction des princes et ses enfans.* Versailles: Impr. du Départ. des affaires étrangeres, 1773.

______. *Maximes fondamentales du gouvernement françois, ou Profession de foi nationale, renfermant tous les dogmes essentiels de notre symbole politique.* Paris: Moutard; Versailles: Blaizot, 1789.

______. *Principes de morale, de politique et de droit public, puisés dans l'histoire de notre monarchie, ou Discours sur l'histoire de France.* 21 vols. Paris: De L'Imprimerie Royale, 1777–1789.

Mounier, Jean Joseph. *De l'influence attribuée aux philosophes, aux frances Maçons et aux illuminés sur la révolution de France.* Paris, 1822.

______. *Recherches sur les causes qui ont empêché les François de devenir libres, et sur les moyens qui leur restent pour acquérir la liberté.* 2 vols. in 1. Geneva, 1792.

Necessité d'une contre-révolution, prouvée par le décret de l'Assemblée prétendue nationale . . . Aux Thuileries, 1790.

Outremont, Anselme d'. *Examen critique de la Révolution françoise considerée comme systeme politique.* London: Cox, 1805.

______. *Le Nouveau siècle ou La France encore Monarchie.* 2 vols. London: De l'imprimerie de Baylis, 1796.

Pawlet, Fleury Paulet. *Pétition de M. de Pawlet, dont l'objet est de démontrer à l'Assemblée nationale que le Roi n'a jamais cessé de désirer le bonheur des Français.* [Paris]: impr. de Girouard [1789].

Peltier, Jean Gabriel. *Le Coup d'équinoxe pour servir de suite à "Sauvez-nous, ou Sauvez-vous", et a "la Trompette du Jugement" [Supplement]* Paris: September 22, 1789.

______. *Dernier Tableau de Paris, ou Récit historique de la Révolution du 10 août 1792, Des Causes qui l'ont produite, des Évenemens qui l'ont précédée, et des Crimes qui l'ont suivie.* 3rd ed. 2 vols. London; Brussels: chez B. Le Francq, April, 1794.

______. *La Trompette du jugement.* Paris: au Sallon d'Hercule, September, 1789.

Protestation de la noblessse de France, émigrée dans les pays étrangers, contre la sanction donnée par le roi à la prétendue charte constitutionnelle. Coblenz, September, 1791.

Réal de Curban, Gaspard de. *La Science du gouvernement.* 8 vols. Aix-la-Chapelle and Paris, [1751?]–1765.

Rivarol, Antoine. *Écrits et pamphlets de Rivarol . . . recueillis pour la première fois et annotés par A. P. Malassis.* Paris: A. Lemerre, 1877.

______. *Rivarol.* Jean Dutourd, ed. [Paris]: Mercure de France [1963].

Rozoi, Barnabé Farmian de. *Royalisme français.* [Paris]: impr. de J. Girouard, n.d.

Sabatier, abbé Antoine [known as de Castres]. *Pensées et observations morales et politiques pour servir à la connaissance des vrais principes du gouvernement.* Vienna: Ignace Alberti, 1794.

Sénac de Meilhan, Gabriel. "Défense de Louis XVI [in 1792], in Louis Hastier, *Vieilles Histoires, étranges énigmes.* 3rd series. Paris: Arthème Fayard, 1960, 51–56.

[Sénac de Meilhan, Gabriel]. *Des principes et des causes de la Révolution en France.* London, 1790.

______. *Du gouvernement, des moeurs, et des conditions en France avant la révolution; avec le caractère des principaux personnages du règne de Louis XVI.* Hamburg: B. G. Hoffmann, 1795.

[Sourdat, Nicolas of Troyes]. *Les Véritables auteurs de la Révolution de France de 1789.* [Neuchâtel]: Les Librairies associés, 1797.

La tête leur tourne: 1788, N.p., 1788.

Tinseau d'Amondans de Gennes, Charles Marie Thérèse Léon. *Nouveau plan de constitution, présenté par MM. les émigrés, à la nation françoise, ou Essai sur les deux déclarations du Roi, Faites le 23 Juin 1789; sur les modifications à y faire pour qu'elles puissent servir de bases au Gouv. François; et sur la necéssité de les proposer le plus promptement possible à l'acceptation des États-Généraux.* Worms; Paris: chez les Marchands de Nouveautés, 1792.

Vaulx, Bernarrd de, ed. *Journal de François Suleau, le chevalier de la difficulté et écrits divers.* Paris: Jacques et René Wittmann, 1946.

Williams, Helen Maria. *Political and Confidential Correspondence of Lewis the Sixteenth.* 3 vols. London: G & J. Robinson, 1803.

BOOKS AND ARTICLES

Aulard, Alphonse. "Les Premiers historiens de la Révolution française—Lacretelle, Toulongeon, Beaulieu, Bertrand de Moleville." *La Révolution française*, 57 (July–December, 1909), 97–136.

Baker, Keith Michael. "Controlling French History: The Ideological Arsenal of Jacob-Nicolas Moreau." Paper presented to the Chicago Group on the History of the Social Sciences, March 15, 1983.

______. "French Political Thought at the Accession of Louis XVI." *Journal of Modern History*, 50 (June, 1978), 279–303.

______."On the Problem of the Ideological Origins of the French Revolution," in Dominick LaCapra and Steven L. Kaplan, eds., *Modern European Intellectual History: Reappraisals and New Perspectives.* Ithaca: Cornell University Press, 1982, 197–219.

Baldensperger, Fernand. *Le movement des idées dans l'émigration française (1789–1815).* 2 vols. Paris: Plon-Nourrit, 1924.

Barbier, Edmond Jean François. *Chronique de la régence et du règne de Louis XV (1718–1763); ou, Journal de Barbier.* 8 vols. Paris: Charpentier, 1857.

Barker, Nancy N. "The Social Interpretation of the French Revolution: Empiricists and Theorists." *Proceedings of the Consortium on Revolutionary Europe*, 17 (1987), 195–208.

Barton, H. A. "The Origins of the Brunswick Manifesto." *French Historical Studies*, 4 (Fall, 1967), 146–69.

Beik, Paul H. "The comte d'Antraigues and the Failure of French Conservatism in 1789." *American Historical Review*, 56 (1951), 767–87.

______. *The French Revolution Seen from the Right: Social Theories in Motion, 1789–1799. Transactions of the American Philosophical Society.* New series, vol. 46, Part 1. Philadelphia, 1956.

Bellanger, Claude, Jacques Godechot, Pierre Guiral, and Fernand Terrou. *Histoire générale de la presse française*. 5 vols. Paris: Presses Universitaires de France, 1969–1975.

Bertaud, Jean Paul. *Les Amis du Roi: Journaux et journalistes royalistes en France de 1789 à 1792*. Paris: Perrin, 1984.

Bertin, Francis. "La monarchie selon les émigrés." *Découverte* (1974), 43–50.

Bertrand, E. "Un ministre de la marine sous Louis XVI: Bertrand de Molleville (*sic*]. *Revue des études historiques*, 97 (1931), 411–30.

Bestermann, T. "Voltaire, Absolute Monarchy and the Enlightened Monarch." *Studies on Voltaire and the Eighteenth Century*, 32 (1965), 7–21.

Bien, David D. "Offices, Corps, and a System of State Credit: The Uses of Privilege under the Ancien Regime," in Keith Michael Baker, ed., *The Political Culture of the Old Regime*. New York: Pergamon Press, 1987, 89–114.

Bonney, Richard. "Absolutism: What's in a Name?" *French History*, 1 (1987), 93–117.

Bossuet, Jacques Bénigne. *Politique tirée des propres paroles de l'Écriture sainte*. Édition critique avec introduction et notes par Jacques Le Brun. Geneva: Librairie Droz, 1967.

Bouloiseau, Marc. *The Jacobin Republic, 1792–1794*. Translated by Jonathan Mandelbaum. Cambridge; New York: Cambridge University Press; Paris: Editions de la Maison des sciences de l'homme, 1983.

Burmeister, Brigitte. "Les paradoxes de Linguet." *Dix–huitième siècle*, (1975), 147–55.

Cavanaugh, Gerald J. "Turgot: The Rejection of Enlightened Despotism." *French Historical Studies*, 6 (Spring 1969), 31–58.

______. "Vauban, d'Argenson, Turgot: From Absolutism to Constitutionalism in Eighteenth-century France," Columbia University Ph.D. dissertation, 1967.

Censer, Jack R. "Reinterpreting the French Revolution: The Search for Intellectual Origins." *Proceedings of the Consortium on Revolutionary Europe*, 17 (1987), 181–94.

Chaumié, Jacqueline. *Le Reseau d'Antraigues et la contre-révolution, 1791–1793*. [Paris]: Plon, 1965.

Chisick, Harvey. "Pamphlets and Journalism in the Early French Revolution: The Offices of the *Ami du Roi* of the Abbé Royou as a Center of Royalist Propaganda." *French Historical Studies*, 15 (Fall 1988), 623–45.

Doyle, William. *The Origins of the French Revolution*. New York: Oxford University Press, 1980.

______. *The Oxford History of the French Revolution*. New York: Oxford University Press, 1989.

Duckworth, Colin. *The D'Antraigues Phenomenon: the Making and Breaking of a Revolutionary Espionage Agent*. Newcastle upon Tyne, England: Averno Publications, Ltd., 1986.

Echeverria, Durand. *The Maupeou Revolution. A Study in the History of Libertarianism: France 1770–1774*. Baton Rouge, London: Louisiana State University Press, 1985.

Escoube, Pierre. *Sénac de Meilhan (1736–1803, De la France de Louis XV à l'Europe des émigrés, Suivi de: Du Gouvernement, des moeurs et des conditions en France, avant la Révolution* (extraits). Paris: Libraire Academique Perrin, 1984.

______. "Un Versaillais méconnu: Sénac de Meilhan (1736–1803), *Revue de l'histoire de Versailles et des Yvelines* 63 (1978), 15–35.

Fitzsimmons, Michael P. "Privilege and the Polity in France, 1786–1791." *American Historical Review* 92 (April 1987), 269–95.

Fryer, Walter Ronald. *Republic or Restoration in France? 1794–7. The Politics of French Royalism, with particular reference to the activities of A. B. J. d'André.* Manchester: Manchester University Press, 1965.

Furet, François. *Interpreting the French Revolution.* Cambridge, New York: Cambridge University Press; Paris: Éditions de la Maison des sciences de l'homme, 1981.

Gay, Peter. *Voltaire's Politics: The Poet as Realist.* Princeton: Princeton University Press, 1959.

Gershoy, Leo. *The French Revolution and Napoleon.* New York: Appleton-Century Crofts, 1933, 1964.

Gilchrist, J. and W. J. Murray, eds. *The Press in the French Revolution: A Selection of Documents taken from the Press of the Revolution for the Years 1789–1794.* New York: St. Martin's Press, 1971.

Godechot, Jacques. *La Contre-révolution. Doctrine et action (1789–1804).* Paris: Presses universitaires de France, 1961.

______. *Les Révolutions, 1770–1799.* Paris: Presses universitaires de France, 1963.

Goldstein, Marc A. *The People in French Counter-Revolutionary Thought.* New York: Peter Lang, 1988.

Gottschalk, Louis. *The Place of the American Revolution in the Causal Pattern of the French Revolution*, Easton, Pa.: American Friends of Lafayette, 1948.

Gruder, Vivian R. "The Bourbon Monarchy: Reforms and Propaganda at the End of the Old Regime," in Keith Michael Baker, ed., *The Political Culture of the Old Regime.* New York: Pergamon Press, 1987, 347–74.

Hartung, F., and R. Mousnier. "Quelques problèmes concernant la monarchie absolute." *X Congresso Internazionale di Science Storiche, Relazioni*, 4 (1955), 1–55.

Hill, Henry Bertram. "French constitutionalism: Old Regime and Revolutionary." *The Journal of Modern History*, 21 (1949), 222–27.

Hudson, David. "In Defense of Reform: French Government Propaganda during the Maupeou Crisis." *French Historical Studies*, 8 (1973), 51–76.

Hunt, Lynn. *Politics, Culture, and Class in the French Revolution.* Berkeley: University of California Press, 1984.

Hutchins, Robert Maynard, ed. *Great Books of the Western World*, vol. 23, Nicolò Machiavelli, *The Prince*, Thomas Hobbes, *Leviathan, or Matter, Form, and Power of a Commonwealth Ecclesiastical and Civil.* Chicago: Encyclopaedia Britannica, Inc., 1952.

Hutt, Maurice. *Chouannerie and Counter-Revolution: Puisaye, the Princes, and the British Government in the 1790s.* 2 vols. New York: Cambridge University Press, 1983.

Johnson, J. A. "Calonne and the Counter-Revolution, 1787–1792." Unpublished Ph.D. thesis, University of London, 1955.

Legg, L. G. Wickham, ed. *Select Documents Illustrative of the French Revolution: the Constituent Assembly.* 2 vols. Oxford: Clarendon Press, 1905.

Lescure, Mathurin F. D. de. *Rivarol et la société française pendant la Révolution et l'émigration (1754–1801), études et portraits historiques et littéraires d'àpres des documents inédits.* Paris: E. Plon, 1883.

Levy, Darliene Gay. *The Ideas and Careers of Simon-Nicolas-Henri Linguet, A Study in Eighteenth-Century French Politics*. Urbana: University of Illinois Press, 1980.

Livois, René de. *Histoire de la presse française*. 2 vols. Paris: Les Temps de la press, 1965.

Lods, Armand. "Un journaliste de la Revolution: le petit Gautier." *La Révolution française*, 63 (1912), 506–12.

Lucas, Colin. "The Rules of the Game in Local Politics under the Directory." *French Historical Studies*, 16 (Fall, 1989), 345–71.

Lyons, Martyn. *France Under the Directory*. London, New York: Cambridge University Press, 1975.

McNeil, Gordon H. "The Anti-Revolutionary Rousseau." *The American Historical Review*, 58 (July 1953), 808–23.

Maspero-Clerc, Hélène. *Un journaliste contre-révolutionnaire, Jean-Gabriel Peltier (1760–1825)*. Paris: Société des Études Robespierristes, 1973.

Mitchell, Harvey. "Counter-revolutionary mentality and popular revolution: two case studies," in J. F. Bosher, *French Government and Society 1500–1800*. London: Athlone Press, 1973, 231–60.

______. "Vendémiaire, a revaluation." *Journal of Modern History*, 30 (1958), 191–202.

Monsembernard, G. de. *Sénac de Meilhan (1736–1803)*. Auch: Th. Bouquet, 1969.

Mornet, Daniel. *Les origines intellectuelles de la Révolution française (1715–1787)*. Paris: Armand Colin, 1933.

Murray, William J. "The Right-Wing Press in the French Revolution (1789–1792). Ph.D. dissertation, Australian National University, 1971.

______. *The Right-Wing Press in the French Revolution: 1789–92*. Woodbridge, Eng.: Boydell & Brewer, 1986.

Neumann, Franz. *The Democratic and the Authoritarian State*. Glencoe, Ill.: Free Press, 1957.

Osen, James L. "Early French Conservatives Explain the Causes of the French Revolution." *Proceedings of the Consortium on Revolutionary Europe*, 15 (1985), 265–80.

______. "French Absolutist Political Thought, 1789–1791." *Proceedings of the Consortium on Revolutionary Europe*, 16 (1986), 21–34.

______. "French Conservative Thought during the Legislative Assembly, 1791–1792." *Proceedings of the Consortium on Revolutionary Europe*, 18 (1988), 95–110.

______. "French Conservatives during Thermidor and the Directory," *Proceedings of the Consortium on Revolutionary Europe*, 19 (1989), vol. II, 95–110.

Palmer, R. R. *The Age of Democratic Revolution. A Political History of Europe and America, 1760–1800*. 2 vols. Princeton: Princeton University Press, 1959–1964.

Pellet, Marcellin. *Un journal royaliste en 1789: "Les Actes des Apôtres" (1789–1791)*. Paris: Armand Le Chevalier, 1873.

Popkin, Jeremy D. "The French Revolutionary Press: New Findings and New Perspectives." *Eighteenth-Century Life*, 51 (Summer 1979), 90–104.

______. *"Joseph Fiévée, imprimeur, écrivain, journaliste; une carrière dans le monde du livre pendant la Révolution," in Livre et Révolution*, Mélanges de la Bibliothèque de la Sorbonne, 9, Frédéric Barbier, Claude Jolly and Sabine Juratic, eds. Paris: Aux Amateurs de Livres, 1989, 63–74.

______. "Journals: The New Face of News," in Robert Darnton and Daniel Roche, eds., *The Press in France, 1775–1800*. Berkeley: University of California Press, 1989, 141–64.

______. *"The Newspaper Press in French Political Thought, 1789– 1799," in Studies in Eighteenth-Century Culture*, 10 (1980), 113–33.

______. *"The Prerevolutionary Origins of Political Journalism," in Keith Michael Baker, ed. The Political Culture of the Old Regime*. New York: Pergamon Press, 1987, 203–223.

______. *Revolutionary News: The Press in France, 1789–1799*. Durham: Duke University Press, 1990.

______. *The Right-Wing Press in France, 1792–1800*. Chapel Hill: University of North Carolina Press, 1980.

______. "The Royalist Press in the Reign of Terror." *The Journal of Modern History*, 51 (December 1979), 685–700.

Reinhard, Marcel. *Religion, révolution et contre-Révolution*. Paris: Les Cours de Sorbonne, 1960.

Rémond, Rene. *La droite en France. De la Première Restauration à la Ve République*. Nouvelle édition revue et augmentée. Paris: Aubier, 1964.

Richet, Denis. "La monarchie au travail sur elle-même?" in Keith Michael Baker, ed., *The Political Culture of the Old Regime*. New York: Pergamon Press, 1987, 25–39.

Roberts, J. M. "The French Origins of the 'Right.'" *Transactions of the Royal Historical Society*, 23 (1973), 27–53.

Roberts, J. M., ed. *French Revolution Documents, Volume I* [1782– 92]. New York: Barnes & Noble, 1966.

Rousseau, Jean Jacques. *Du Contrat social*. Edited with an Introduction and Notes by Ronald Grimsley. Oxford: Clarendon Press, 1972.

______. *The Social Contract and Discourses*. Translation and Introduction by G. D. H. Cole. Revised and augmented by J. H. Brumfitt and John C. Hall. London: J. M. Dent & Sons Ltd., 1973.

See, Henri. *L'Évolution de la pensée politique en France au XVIIIe siècle*. Paris: Giard, 1925.

Sewell, William H., Jr. "Ideologies and Social Revolutions: Reflections on the French Case." *Journal of Modern History*, 57 (1985), 57–85.

Stone, Bailey. "The Geopolitical Origins of the French Revolution Reconsidered," *Proceedings of the Consortium on Revolutionary Europe*, 18 (1988), 250–62.

Tackett, Timothy. *Religion, Revolution, and Regional Culture in Eighteenth Century France: The Ecclesiastical Oath of 1791*. Princeton: Princeton University Press, 1986.

Thompson, J. M., ed. *French Revolution Documents 1789–1794*. Oxford: Basil Blackwell, 1948.

Tourneux, Maurice. "Le régime de la presse de 1789 à l'an VIII." *La Révolution française*, 25 (1893), 193–213.

______. "Trois journaux de Paris pendant la Révolution: 'le Journal des états généraux,' 'le Courrieur français,' 'l'Ami du Roi.'" *La Révolution française*, 58 (1892), 155–75, 269–82.

Van Kley, Dale. "The Jansenist Constitutional Legacy in the French Pre-Revolution." *Historical Reflections/Réflexions historiques*, 13 (1986), 393–453.

______. *The Jansenists and the Expulsion of the Jesuits from France*. New Haven: Yale University Press, 1975.

______. "New Wine in Old Wineskins: Continuity and Rupture in the Pamphlet Debate of the French Prerevolution, 1787–1789." *French Historical Studies*, 17 (Fall 1991), 446–65.

Vielwahr, André. *La Vie et l'oeuvre de Sénac de Meilhan*. Paris: A. G. Nizet, 1970.

Vovelle, Michel. *[The French Revolution I]: The Fall of the French Monarchy 1787–1792*. Cambridge: Cambridge University Press, 1984.

Vyverberg, Henry. "Limits of Nonconformity in the Enlightenment: The Case of Simon-Nicolas-Henri Linguet," *French Historical Studies*, 4 (Fall, 1970), 474–91.

Walter, Gérard, ed. *La Révolution française vue par ses journaux*. Paris: Tardy [1948].

Woronoff, Denis. *The Thermidorean Regime and the Directory, 1794–1799*. Translated by Julian Jackson. Cambridge, New York: Cambridge University Press; Paris: Éditions de la Maison des Sciences de l'Homme, 1984.

Index

About the Author

JAMES L. OSEN is Professor of History at Beloit College.

ISBN 0-313-29441-0
90000>
EAN
9 780313 294419
HARDCOVER BAR CODE